Watercolor Memories

The Story of Lauren

by Brian Wilson

Acknowledgements

It's all WABC's fault!

The original scribblings of *Watercolor Memories: The Story of Lauren* first hit paper in May, 1981 after my partner and I had been brought in to do morning drive on WABC/NY radio. Being back in the metro area for the first time since 1964, I was inundated with memories of growing up on the Wilson Farm in Wayne, New Jersey (when there were still farms there), of childhood, adolescence, school and especially high school where The Story began. So I would like to thank IBM for marketing the PC which I purchased at ComputerLand for a mere $3,000. The Story would never have been written if technology had left me to contend with my Olympia portable typewriter and gallons of Wite Out®. Professional Write and subsequent word-processing software provided a quantum leap forward in my writing efforts. I still get thank-you cards from trees across America having been spared as a result of newly-found Paper Consumption Reduction.

Since '81, *Watercolor Memories: The Story of Lauren* crashed into oblivion and was re-born countless times as lightening, power surges and good old stupidity polished off hard drive content in several subsequent machines. Eventually, a rudimentary "finished copy" was produced and Publishers rejected it without hesitation. Looking back, I can't fault them; the story was clunky, wordy and "a difficult read." A movie treatment was presented to several Hollywood studios by close friends and writers, Fred and Mickey Janney (RIP) who did so despite telling me my simple little tale – as written – sucked; the studios concurred.

After all this rejection, The Story loitered on my last surviving hard drive for several years. Nevertheless, whenever I would tell it to an unsuspecting audience, usually of one or less, the reaction was always very favorable and I was enthusiastically encouraged to turn it into something approaching a novel. Here it is; although more a "novella", I'm told . . .

It never would have made it this far had it not been for that first IBM PC and its progeny, the unvarnished assessment of Fred and Mickey and, years later, Ohio movie magnate Rich Iott. But it was the latter day interest, encouragement, fact-finding and occasional butt-kicks of Ingrid Allex Fox, Paula Thibodeau-Hirsch and Christine Swanson Villani (all WHS Class of '63) who pushed Completion over the Finish Line. That said, they must also share all future blame.

Every worthwhile project has one essential, indispensable individual who selflessly pours out their talent, sacrifices their time, buries personal opinion, all for the sake of The Work. Without them, projects would be left to molder in a jumble of bits and bytes. For *Watercolor Memories: The Story of Lauren*, that one essential, indispensable, "singular sensation", is my Editor, Cassie (Carol Anne) Wilson. Not only did she salvage this piece from contextual Armageddon, she had the unimaginable load of also being married to the over-sensitive author, guarding his precious work from the ravages of an Eagle-Eye Blue Pencil Editor cum Long-Suffering Wife. Not to mention the appalling notion of a wife who would willingly edit the true story of her husband's First Love! Maybe that will be a book she will write one day, guaranteed to be a Best Seller in the Improbable Non-Fiction Category.

-BMW

Contents

Brian Wilson
WHS Class of '63

The Story of Lauren Starts Here

In the beginning . . . once upon a time . . . in a galaxy long ago and far away, it was the best of times, it was the worst of times, it was the age of wisdom, it was the age of foolishness, it was the epoch of belief, it was the spring of hope, it was the winter of despair -- and that was one helluva run-on sentence!

Let's get started. First, everything you're about to read is true. I fell in love with Lauren May 28, 1961, on a blind date to the "Roaring Twenties" dance in our high school gym. At this juncture, a pause for some background may be in order.

In 1961, I'm 16 years old. I had been living away from my home in Wayne, New Jersey for the better part of three years attending one of those "All-Boy-Tie-and-Jacket" New England prep schools, like the one you've seen in *Scent of a Woman*. My parents had decided the local public school system sucked big time, so they determined my newly-discovered elevated IQ needed cultivation at a superior learning institution. Or maybe they just wanted me out of the house. There is evidence to suggest that may have actually been the primary motive. Hell, I had been surrounded for three years by lots of guys who were there for that very reason!

Skipping over the uncomfortable parts of being shuttled off for months at a time to a boarding school two states away, living with people you didn't know in a place you'd never been, things went along just swimmingly until my father's business hit an economic brick wall in 1960. With tuition rivaling that of some small colleges, prep school was no longer an affordable option. Arrangements were made for me to return to the lobotomizing clutches of the Wayne Township Public School System.

It was awkward.

The kids I had grown up with through elementary school hadn't seen me since seventh grade and, of course, had no idea where I went or what happened to me; rumors ran the gauntlet from "dead" to "prison". (Those were some free-floating imaginations for kids in a small town back then.) My sudden appearance after Spring Break caused a mild stir but the ripples died down pretty quickly. More importantly, during my absence, pre-adolescent affiliations sustained everyone heading into puberty and solidified into various identity circles. Having been *in absentia* during this social gestation period, I wasn't part of any clique or klatch nor was I invited to be nor did I expect to be.

This was no big deal. Really. I had no reason to anticipate anything else. The way Wayne was laid out back then, social groupings spontaneously generated via geography more than anything else. If you lived at Packanack Lake, not that far from our farm but outside the formal parameters of the "lake community", you were definitely *not* part of the "lake society". And the "lake society" had some pretty stringent rules, barring anyone not a Resident of "the lake" from participating in any of the social functions sponsored by the "lake society" -- with the exception of Boy Scouts, Girl Scouts and (after some effort) Little League. There were similar communities within Wayne's mostly agricultural 27 square miles: Pines Lake, Lionshead Lake, all with similar restrictive covenants. As New Yorkers made their exodus to the newly-discovered 'Burbs, each area built its own elementary school. But after sixth grade, wherever you lived, everybody funneled into the Anthony Wayne Junior High School and Melting Pot. Here you not only learned the joy of changing classrooms and teachers for different subjects at different periods, more importantly, you discovered there were all these other kids your age who had been living within a few miles of you for the last 12 years! Except for those in your Scout troop or on opposing Little League teams, you had no clue they even existed; that is, unless you were part of a "lake society". If you were raised on a chicken farm, unattached to any identifiable area, you were pretty much on your own.

Or on a tractor.

I mention this now to give you a sense of the social fabric wrapped around me like swaddling clothes at the advanced age of 15 and why, despite being born and raised in one of Wayne's earliest families, it was almost as if I was just as much a "New Boy" as I had been my first year away at prep school.

But I digress . . .

After the initial titters of curiosity and surprise upon my return, things calmed down quickly enough and life became just as big a snoozer as it had been whenever I had come home for the holidays. Living in what was still "the country", both parents working 35 miles away in Manhattan, without serious public transportation, parental transportation, filial transportation or even the distractions of a condensed, self-sustaining "lake community" -- and especially without the coveted all-liberating driver's license -- it was definitely not "the best of times".

I'm a little fuzzy on how everything initially came about but one spring afternoon in May, Rich Lambert, a Wayne High School senior who had dated my big sister a few times (before she determined he was "beneath her"), pulled into the farm when he saw me out mowing on the tractor. His "steady", Ann, was sitting right next to him, his high school ring around her neck, her arm over his shoulder in accordance with the Official 1960's Dating Customs Handbook. After the appropriate small talk, he asked, "Would you be interested in going on a blind date to the "Roaring Twenties" dance in the gym Saturday?" Before I could say anything, Ann jumped in -- the girl's name was Lauren. She lived next door to Ann and they lived just a few miles away (the other side of Route 23, Wayne's outback and gateway to Pequannock, a bedroom community often embarrassingly mispronounced). Predictably, Ann painted a picture of a "very cute" girl, also a sophomore and "a little shy" -- which I took to mean "this is why she doesn't have a date". I remember wondering how could she could live so close, be so cute and I have no clue who she was? That's when I gave myself the 1960s equivalent of today's "face palm". Duh! You've been gone for three years, Genius. Based on how the

Township school district lines were drawn, we wouldn't have attended the same school until Melting Pot Junior High, which of course, was right when I left for Preppyville.

So? So . . . what the hell? Why not?

Magic Saturday and 6:30 arrived and so did Rich and Ann who picked me up and off we went to Lauren's place. The dance organizers were serious about the "Roaring Twenties" theme. Rich was wearing a sports jacket with the widest lapels I had ever seen outside of an old gangster movie, a wide, gaudy tie and a fedora that must have come over on the Ark. Ann was in a sleek black sheath "Flapper" number with lots of not-really pearls around her neck. I was totally out of costume in your basic tie-and-blazer; I didn't think the theme meant all *this* – but it did. Too late now. Even if I had something to change into, we would have been unacceptably late. No need to make a bad First Impression; blind dates are hard enough.

Naturally, this was going to involve enduring the dreaded "Meet the Parents and Squirm" Ordeal. While a tad apprehensive, I was reasonably confident my Amy Vanderbilt-inspired prep school-infused manners would get me through the pending inquisition. And it wasn't as if I had never been on a date before. There was the Dance Class Graduation Dance in fifth grade with Barbara Sasse whose tooth I had knocked out, kissing her on a dare in fourth grade. Such a romantic! What I lacked in finesse, I made up with enthusiasm; a regular Romeo cum Marquis de

Sade rolled into one otherwise reasonably well-mannered pre-teeny-bopper package. But that had been *years* ago! I had matured.

In a 10 -15 minute drive from the farm, we're pulling into Lauren's driveway. Rich and Ann led the way to the front door of a modest green shingle ranch house with tall trees all around. I had ridden past this place on the way to Pequannock hundreds of times. Who could have thought then what was about to happen now, not to mention what lied ahead? A child's playground set was in the fenced backyard; Lauren had siblings.

Prep school manners notwithstanding, I've always hated introductions: the meaningless how-do-you-do's, aimless small talk, dull or pointed questions. But Lauren's mom was a charmer; friendly, warm, pleasant and a great laugh. She promptly confirmed I was *the* Brian Wilson from the Wilson Farm. Sometime, somewhere, she remembered meeting my mother and that took care of my vetting. Lauren's father greeted me with all the warmth and sincerity of any father convinced my only reason for living was to get in his daughter's pants as expeditiously as time, space and opportunity would allow. Thanks to being cloistered in prep school for three of my formative years, I was too inexperienced to be up on the latest Dating Policies, Practices, and Procedures, but I noodled out that Lauren's conspicuous absence was just a necessary part of the ceremony setting me up for her "Grand Entrance".

I was not disappointed. Even in its simplicity, Lauren's entrance was, indeed, very, *very* "Grand".

The Date

The Sills lived in a green split-level house on Black Oak Ridge Road, almost on a straight line a few miles west of the Wilson farm. It was the kind of floor plan where all the important rooms were on the first floor; upstairs were a couple of bedrooms and a bath. As you came in the front door, you were immediately in the living room. The stairs were to the left, open halfway up to where the ceiling began and parallel to where we were all standing. While waiting for Lauren's appearance, Mr. Sills mostly ignored me, chatting instead with Rich. Mrs. Sills was going on with Ann about her outfit. Lauren's little sister – (*did I mention the little sister?*) was doing those little annoying things little sisters do when their big sisters are going out on a date; everyone milling about in classic Hurry Up And Wait mode.

You will note on my resume I never won any awards for patience.

In a lull in the buzz of conversation, the sound of a heel on wood and 12 eyes turned as one to the visible portion of the stairs. More step sounds, then black pumps and slender ankles appeared. Lauren. Then came very nice calves and knees wrapped in black nylon stockings (I think nylon; no awards for Women's Fashion savvy either). Then black fringe along the hem of a dark red satin sheath dress. Then waist, bodice, neckline and . . .

this beautiful face with a dazzling smile! Lauren! Her eyes swept over Rich and Ann, her mother (still at the foot of the stairs), and to her father. Then they found me, standing a little apart from everyone else. She smiled right into my eyes. And hundreds of thousands of sparkling lights filled the room all at once.

Over the years, I'm sure I have forgotten many things, big and small, about Lauren. Yet nothing short of a full-blown frontal lobotomy could erase my memory of that moment, that setting and that magnificent smile that transformed her from Really Attractive to Breathlessly Stunning.

Like most of the girls in our sophomore class, Lauren brought all the standard factory equipment. Her hair was short, styled sort of – (*what?*) "pixie-ish"? Maybe for the theme of the dance? Couldn't be sure; I was still trying to get my eyesight back.

Mrs. Sills, "You look lovely, dear!"
Ann, "What a cute outfit; I love it!"
Rich, "Hey! Wow! Nice!"
Mr. Sills, "Very nice, honey."
Brian . . . Crickets.

What could I say? We hadn't even been introduced yet!

That little technicality seemed to hit Ann, Rich and Mrs. Sills simultaneously as they all at once started talking, "Brian-this-is-Hey-

Lauren-this-is-Wil-I-Brian-here-is-would-like-want-to-you-to-meet-say-Wilson-my-Lauren-daughter-meet-you."

Did I mention I hated introductions?

Lauren and her smile just floated across the space between us. Looking up at me, she said in a clear, soft voice, "I know . . . Hi."

"Hi!" With a dopey-loopy grin from the normally-loquacious-now-suddenly-monosyllabic Brian "Mumbles" Wilson.

I remember thinking, *there really is a God! How could I be this lucky?*

We left with the usual cacophony of "Have-A-Good-Time-Don't-Be-Too-Late-Drive-Carefully-Nice-To-Meet-You-Yes-Me   Too-Right-Fine-Sure-OK" and headed to the school in a cloud of small talk. Once inside the sparsely decorated, dimly lit gym, Rich and Ann soon wandered off with friends giving Lauren and me our first chance to talk with just each other. Without actually saying so, we both were happy just walking and talking rather than sitting or dancing. We dealt with the interruptions from her friends, Judy, Joan and several others who made the obligatory drive-by "inspection", eventually followed by the compulsory Girl's Room Stampede. She surprised me with the stories "everyone" had been telling about me my first days back -- I had been in jail, in a hospital or had run away from home -- all made the rounds. Not knowing me or anything about me, she admitted she was curious about "the real story". I gave her the condensed version of my parents "Public School vs. Prep School" issues and all the dots connected. We talked about our families and school, who we had for what classes and what we wanted to be when we grew up (she -- Art Teacher, me -- Clarence Darrow), and other stuff adolescent conversation is made of. We danced the slow dances, of course.

Throughout the evening, I was just trying to be cool enough to send her the message that for me, this had turned into a really great evening. The last thing I wanted was to say or do anything that would turn her off or scare her away. I had no big reason to feel anxious; just the standard Free-Floating Adolescent Anxieties. I wasn't all that sure of myself with this social construct either. Not "shy" per se, just your basically insecure teenage guy, astounded that this remarkably attractive girl was here with me. **ME**! I wanted to be cool but not a cliché; to impress her but not sure how to, or how hard I should try, or if I had already blown it and she was just being polite. Yes, there was That Smile back at her house, but maybe she was just being nice. Even if I had conjured up something "impressive" to say or do, I wouldn't have, fearing failure and rejection. For all the euphoria in that moment, I felt like a guy juggling a bowling ball, a chainsaw and an egg. So I did what I always did and took cover behind my faithful, impenetrable shield and resource: humor. And I was rewarded throughout the evening with Lauren's dazzling smile and soft, spontaneous laughter. I even scored an Elusive Giggle!

It soon became clear Lauren didn't deserve Ann's earlier "shy" label. She had no reticence in speaking as frankly and openly as could be expected at that point -- (*an hour?*) into our "relationship". She laughed easily and always "got it". She was an excellent dancer which probably explained why she did so well on the Flag Twirling Squad and Girls Gymnastics Team over the next two years. She carried herself confidently, comfortably with no self-consciousness. She had no reason to. If she had any reservations of self-esteem or insecurity, they weren't on display. She wasn't shy; she just wasn't a Type "A" personality like her date.

While I may have "never met a stranger" when it came to the Opposite Sex, I had my hang-ups: my big brother, Craig, was 6'1", slender, with our father's blue eyes, light brown curly hair and a Varsity Basketball star. With impeccable taste in clothes, if GQ had been published back then he could have been on the cover; girls noticed when he walked into the room. His date to the prom could have been Miss June 1959. I grew up in his shadow at the Polar Opposite Pole; my clothes were purchased in the Husky Department. Fighting as kids, he could easily outrun me. On the rare occasion I caught him, I'd get him down on the ground and beat the living crap out of him. On the upside, his smuggled copies of Playboy, cleverly hidden under his mattress in our shared bedroom where Mom never ever found them, provided my early introduction to the marvels of the Naked Woman. Seeing some of the beauties he dated, my pubescent logic concluded a guy had to look like *him* to get dates with women like *them.* Without his unquestionably good looks, sartorial expertise and that Varsity Letter, I was to be perpetually Down One when considering a relationship with the opposite sex.

And so with Lauren that evening, while confident of my "social graces", I suffered a serious Confidence Deficit hovering over the evening. The ghost of my brother's b-ball prowess haunted the very gym floor we danced on. At 16, Lauren may not have had the fuselage of Miss June but if Smile, Poise, and Personality could be measured, she was already 36-24-36. I could only hope I wouldn't do something terminally stupid.

In 1961, for teenagers fighting the War on Puberty, holding hands and good-night kisses were a Very. Big. Deal. Every week in the *Paterson Evening News,* there were letters to *Dear Abby* from some teeny-bopper with a twist on the raging debate "Do I Kiss Him Goodnight on the First Date?" While there were times taking your date's hand was just good manners, physical contact was usually broken as soon as the dance was over -- unless you were in some committed relationship like Rich and Ann "going steady". Whatever -- that was my understanding of the "Rules of Engagement" circa 1961, mildly distorted by White Anglo-Saxon Protestant upbringing, vestiges of Victorian morality and Proper Prep School Paranoia. Anything more assertive would likely have been interpreted as "unwelcome pressure" and I sure as hell wasn't going to risk that.

That's why what happened next was so amazing!

The dance was over and we were walking to Rich's car when, for no identifiable reason, Lauren simply reached out and took my hand, as if it was just the right and natural thing to do! I responded with my best imitation of "Cool Nonchalance" and held her hand back. In the back seat riding back to her place, Lauren kept right on holding my hand, sitting right next to me just like Ann sat right next to Rich. We all talked and laughed about the dance and the crazy outfits and things we had seen, who was doing what with whom. To this day, I cannot figure out why in 1961, there was a "Roaring Twenties" dance for high school kids. Our parents weren't that old. They didn't even have a Charleston contest like the one in *It's a Wonderful Life*! I do know I was feeling pretty damn happy someone had the idea to do something that created this evening for me to be here holding hands with Lauren.

After Rich pulled into the driveway, we sat in the car a while longer, talking and laughing, just having a great time! Rich and Ann got into a little argument about something about a couple they knew that had nothing to do with Lauren or me. So, disengaged from the back-and-forth between them and us, Lauren looked up at me with that smile and said, "Thank you, I had a really great time tonight!" Then *she* kissed *me*! Now according to the RoE in 1961, girls didn't make a habit of initiated kisses, especially on the First Date! Girls were supposed to wait with some measure of feigned reluctance until the guy made the first move. Then, the Girl could Dodge, Weave and Avoid or Surrender and Participate, choosing her personal Level of Enthusiasm. Lauren's kiss was not some little "peck". It wasn't Tonsil Hockey either. I remember her lips were light, soft, gentle but with an unmistakable excitement and enthusiasm and pressing on mine signaling she *wanted* to be kissing me! This was not charity or gratitude or "what's expected". It was spontaneous, on the cutting edge of 1961 decorum! A warm, moist, lingering kiss that lasted not too long, not too short. It was simply Perfect.

I walked her to the door and we talked a little more about what a great time it was and maybe we could meet at school Monday since we didn't know each other's schedules and we didn't ride the same bus and when we agreed to all that and there was nothing left to say and we were at her door. She looked up at me, stood on her toes, put her arms around my neck and kissed me again. Perfectly. She came down off her toes, smiled That Smile and in a soft, clear voice said, "Goodnight" and turned to the door.

"Is-it-OK-if-I-call-you-tomorrow?" I asked, setting a new World Speed Talking Record.

She turned, still smiling, "Yes!" And she was gone.

I know I made it back to the car. I'm just not sure exactly how.

Dinner and a Picnic

Rich and Ann peppered me with questions all the way back to the farm.

"Well? Did you have a good time?"

"Looked like a kiss goodnight from here . . ."

"Do you like her?"

"What did you talk about?"

"Are you going to ask her out?"

"Isn't she cute?"

"Yes-yes-it-was-of-course-everything-nothing-yes-very-sure."

As newly-minted matchmakers, they had a vested interest. I was, of course, most grateful!

"Thanks-for-the-ride-welcome-thanks-a   lot-see-you-Monday-yeah-right-sure-cool-OK."

And off they went.

Once inside, I tried to sneak past the inevitable Parental Post Date Debriefing that would take place in the living room where the folks were watching TV. I could get to the stairs without going through the LR if I could just get passed my mother's radar ears. No such luck . . .

"So did you have a good time*?*" (*Fantastic!*)

"Yeah. Fine. It was OK."

"Is Lauren a nice girl?" (*No, she has warts and smells like a wet goat.*)

"Yes, yes . . . very nice."

"Did you meet her parents?" (*No, she's an orphan being raised in a double-wide by a she-wolf and two Italian kids.*)

"Yes. Mrs. Sills said she had met you somewhere some time ago."

"What does her father do?" (*He owns a Q-tip recycling plant.*)

"I dunno know. It didn't come up."

"Well, what did you talk about?" (*The usual, how my parents are nosey Communist spies who sell drugs to third graders.*)

"The usual . . . school and music and stuff."

"Would you like to invite her over for dinner sometime?" (*Actually, she's in the kitchen waiting for breakfast.*)

"Sure. How about tomorrow?"

"Tomor . . . ? Oh, Brian! You're so silly sometimes!"

"Well, I guess I get that way when I'm exhausted from my whirlwind social life. All these late hours, dancing and drinking and carousing. You know how it is. I'm gonna hit the sack."

"Ha-ha-ha! Funny! Good night, dear."

Yeesh.

No biggie. My parents' Third Degree was not going to be a buzz kill! Her perfume was still on my shirt. At some point, I drifted off while re-re-re-re-playing the evening as visions of Lauren danced in my head.

And so it began.

I waited until around 3:30 Sunday afternoon to make the call. One of the things we hadn't talked about who went where or did what on Sundays. Since 3:30 was generally the time we both got home from school, 3:30 seemed safe and appropriate.

Still swimming in the memories from the night before, I dialed her number. Of course, happy-go-lucky Mr. Sills answered.

"Hello?" (*Ah . . . all the warmth gathered from the last Ice Age!*)
"Hi, Mr. Sills, it's Brian Wilson. (Silence) We met last evening? (Silence) Before the dance. (Silence) (*You know – where I tore off Lauren's dress, just behind the bleachers? She must have mentioned it.*) May I speak with Lauren, please?"
(Pause) (*Was he really thinking about saying No?*)
"Hold on . . . Lauren, it's for you . . ." (*If that guy laid a hand on you last night, why I'll . . .*)

Lauren was there in a heartbeat. I know this because I was counting mine.

"Hello!" I could actually feel her smiling through the phone. She sounded slightly out of breath as if she had been laughing.
"Well! What's so darn funny?" I demanded in my best basso profundo voice.
Taken slightly aback, she said, "Nothing! Why?"
"Well, it sounded as if you were laughing."
"No! I knew it was going to be you and I'm just happy you called!"
The phone and I melted simultaneously.

"Oh, right . . . um . . . well . . . me too!" (*How original! And clever, too! Brian and the Blind Stammers playing for your conversational enjoyment this afternoon!*)

We talked about nothing for an hour. "Do you like . . . Have you seen . . . Did you ever . . . What's your favorite . . . Don't you hate . . . Don't you love . . . ?"

Yes, even as teenagers, we were capable of great depth and deep thought. Time took on another dimension. Turns out we had been yapping for almost two hours when Lauren's mom called her to dinner at 5:30!

"Let's meet near the Senior Door tomorrow; I'll walk you to homeroom."
"Yes! Great! OK! See you then. Bye!"
"Bye!"

And so, our Morning Routine began at 8:05 the next morning. It still bummed me out the school bus routes were just as bizarre as the school district boundaries. It was a much easier, shorter, direct route from Lauren's to the farm to the school than the route her bus or mine actually took. This was my first lesson in Government Planning and Bureaucratic Efficiency. Robbed of the joy of another 20 minutes – no, 40 minutes! -- to *and* from school each day made it 200 minutes lost per week! Someone needed to be held accountable! This was a conspiracy! I began to suspect maybe Mr. Sills worked for the Board of Education.

Most every morning we would meet across from the Senior Door -- which just so happened to be next to the Principal's Office -- and I'd get to start my day with a Lauren Smile. She was in Mrs. Harding's homeroom, a moderate hike from the Senior Door that took a tad longer if you walked slowly. I didn't know it at the time but according to the RoE in 1961: *Daily Walking a Girl to her Locker and/or Homeroom is a major part of the Dating Experience and an Important First Step in establishing the Established Relationship.*

Not sharing any classes, separate Lunch periods, separate buses, our Established Relationship would be taking longer to "establish" than whatever was considered normal. With the Final Bell at 2:30, I would do some of the best broken-field running ever seen off a high school football field getting to Lauren's locker to walk her to the bus. If I could get there before she closed and locked her door, we'd have a few extra minutes -- assuming no body-blocks along the way.

This would be very important later.

We would walk and talk about the day; she'd say hi to smiling *nudge-nudge-wink-wink* friends. When all went well, we'd have about 20 minutes together. She'd always be the last one on the bus. Right after I got home, I'd give her a call and we'd yap another 20 minutes. About what? Who knows? Stuff! Not having shared the same Elementary School Experience, the same neighborhood or the same anything else, we had years of things to talk about and discover. Time was irrelevant. Being with Lauren was my Daily Miracle.

Two weeks after the dance, just before school was out for the summer, Mrs. Sills invited me over for a Saturday night dinner with the family. This was my first Approach-Avoidance Conflict. Yes, anything that meant more time with Lauren. No, I don't think I could handle an entire evening with Mr. Sills' cheery disposition. "Approach" won.

Dad dropped me off. I was all gussied up in overkill, wearing my best preppy tie-and-jacket outfit. Of course, the Sills family observed Saturday Nite Casual, which made me look like a teenage insurance salesman. In what may have been an unannounced test of table manners and culinary craft, Mrs. Sills had prepared chicken and spaghetti for the evening's epicurean repast, a dish that challenges the deft deployment of all available utensils while simultaneously exposing family eating customs. Chicken: with or without fingers? Spaghetti: with or without Large Spoon Pasta Twirling Shield? Cut-up or "in strand"? Dangling End Sucking or No Dangling End Sucking? It was the Ultimate Dining-Cum-Table-Manners Challenge!

Fortunately, Lauren's little sister was so caught up with having company for dinner (and food she could play with as well as eat), she provided sufficient distraction for Mr. and Mrs. Sills' "Wallpaper Protection" efforts which, in turn, prevented me from being too critically inspected. (My free-floating insecurities were rapidly morphing into adolescent paranoia.) Still, it was a good meal and a fun time despite the hovering dark clouds rumbling over Mr. Sills' end of the table. Having told Lauren several times my observations and concerns about her father – to her consistent denial – his countenance became one of those Glance and Giggle routines between us whenever he was around. Fortunately, we maintained sufficient self-control to not arouse any "What Are You Two Laughing About"-isms.

And then it was June 23rd!

School's out for summer. Bummer! Summer vacation meant no school. No school meant no Lauren. It would be another 10 months before I turned 17, the magical age the Garden State deemed you worthy of the Key to Freedom: the coveted Driver's License! Without one, transportation was at the mercy of parents, brothers, sisters or friends. Rich and Ann were having frequent Trouble in Paradise so double-dating was not always an option; being picked up/dropped off by parents was Totally kah-kah. (See *The Karate Kid.*)

Shortly after the 4th of July, calling Lauren for our daily chat, she greeted me with, "Hey! How would you like to go on a picnic with us? We're going up to Ringwood Manor this Saturday and Mom asked if you'd like to come. Would you?"

"Wait... your mom wants to take me on a picnic to Ringwood Manor?"

Home Run -- The Lauren Laugh!

"No! I'm asking!

"Who all is coming along?"

"Everyone."

"Your sister?

"Yes! Of course!"

"Annnnnd . . . ?"

She burst out laughing again at the Hanging Insinuation.

"YES! Daddy's coming, too!"

More laughs on both phones.

"Have you ever been there?"

"Oh yeah. Went up there on a field trip back in sixth grade and again with my Boy Scout patrol on a camping thing before I went off to prep school. Nice place if you like Revolutionary War cannons and old houses."

Ringwood Manor, Site of Revolutionary War Significance, is preserved in a gorgeous park-like setting sprawled over 500 acres in North Jersey, 30 miles from Wayne and a mere cannonball shot from the New York State line. There was the preserved Manor House, tall old oak trees, large ponds and running streams, including one that made a small waterfall as it emptied into the main pond. On the other side, another stream running out of the pond gurgled down through the official Picnic Area. There were a few old cannons scattered here and there, a reminder to visitors what this place was all about once upon a time. And there were walking trails and paths which wove in and out of the surrounding woods. I thought – hoped -- Lauren and I would get a chance to lose her family and spend some time wandering in those woods, on those paths, together. *Alone.*

Everything was set. My brother would drop me off at the Sills' house; they would drop me off back at the farm. While I wasn't supremely comfortable with the arrangement -- 30 minutes in the car with Mr. Warmth and Lauren's little perpetual motion noise machine -- but it was 30 minutes with Lauren whom I hadn't seen in three weeks, an eternity by any reasonable teenage standard.

Saturday arrived bright, blue and just warm enough. The trip to Ringwood was actually pleasant. Mr. Sills concentrated on navigating their powder blue Ford station wagon, little sister wedged between mom and dad totally eliminated the Backseat Stare. Lauren and her mother dominated most of the conversation, drawing me in occasionally for comic relief. Once we arrived, found the Picnic Area with a table in a shady spot near the "bold stream", everything became a pleasant blur of unloading, unpacking, tidying up some debris from some less fastidious picnickers, lighting the charcoal and laying out the goodies. Surprisingly, Mr. Sills turned out to be a pretty good burger flipper. The sun was warm, the humidity low and the breeze just enough to move the leaves and keep the smoke from other grills blowing in the right direction.

After the burgers and hot dogs and potato salad and pickles and chips and dips and Cokes disappeared, we all policed the area. As soon as we finished, Lauren's sister scampered off to throw sticks and watch them zip down the nearby stream to Lake Oblivion and beyond; Mom and Dad dutifully followed. Lauren and I seized the chance to wander off and finally be by ourselves.

The way time bends and blends fact with fantasy into a blurry mosaic, I have few crystal-clear memories of us together, but this is one of them. We never made it to the paths and the woods as I had imagined. Instead, we wandered up to an enormous willow tree on the bank overlooking the biggest of the ponds, just down from the great Manor House. We found a perfect spot against its trunk where two teenagers could sit together and take in the panorama of fields, pond, and Manor House without turning. So there we sat. As usual, I did most of the talking, Lauren did most of the smiling. And we held hands. And even kissed again. While that was over 50 years ago, when the summer sun is just right, the smell of freshly cut grass hangs in the air and a perfect breeze all come together as they did that afternoon, I don't even have to close my eyes; I am back to that very spot in that very moment, under the canopy of that huge willow tree, holding hands with Lauren. There couldn't have been a more perfect day for anyone anywhere. I will never recall what those superb cookies were that Mrs. Sills brought that day or the great joke Mr. Sills actually told on the way home, but the memory of us together, leaning back against that old tree, holding hands is as vivid and indelible as the evening of Lauren's First Smile.

Thinking about the way things are today among 16-year-olds, I should tell you here that our relationship was quite chaste. In fact, it never crossed my mind that Lauren and I would ever . . . well, you know. It wasn't as if we were oblivious to sex; it just wasn't something you *did* at 16 back then. Kissing? Sure. But "second base" and beyond was for the Big Leagues, maybe a few years later. Even if we had been mutually inclined, opportunity was never pounding on the door. When you're being chauffeured around by one of your parents, it's not as if you can say, "Hey Mom! Pull over, will ya? Lauren and I want to get it on!"

Without the coveted driver's license, we would only see each other a couple more times that summer but we talked most every day; sometimes for a few minutes, sometimes for an hour learning bits and pieces about each other. Nothing monumental. Just those little things that grow into bigger things that grow into an Established Relationship.

I never thought I would be happy school was starting! But without the coveted NJ DL, relying on Anyone Else for transportation, summer had become a huge drag. And Lauren Abstinence was driving me nuts!

Opening Day! And we got right back into The Old Routine. We still didn't ride the same bus or have any classes together. Or even Lunch Period! (I was now convinced Mr. Sills was behind this.) But it was going to be a Great Year! We were Juniors! We would be getting our Graduation Rings. And there was the Junior-Senior Prom. Of course, there were the fall football games but Lauren was a Flag Twirler so, while she looked great out there doing her flag thing in her uniform and all, she had to stay with the squad throughout the game. On away games, she was – away. Time was flying by. We managed some double-dates with the reunited Rich and Ann and there was the school Christmas Dance. While spring was still months away, come April I would turn 17 and the long-awaited driver's license would be mine! Meanwhile, we would meet at the Senior Door and walk to Lauren's homeroom; at 2:30, from homeroom back to the bus then the afternoon phone call.

Repeat. Life was good.

Alfred Lord Tennyson wrote, "In spring, a young man's heart turns to Love." Lord Alfred E. Neuman (no relation) wrote, "Come spring and a young man's brain turns to sap." It may have been a tad premature for spring sap, but I determined the time had arrived to make the leap to that Established Relationship and ask Lauren to Go Steady!

Going Steady

Everything anyone wanted to know about "Going Steady" was sung by Elvis Presley: *Wear My Ring Around Your Neck* in 1958. The lyrics were dutifully memorized mostly by teenage girls and remained valid until Woodstock changed everything. In any high school, it was a Very. Big. Deal. It even had its own set of "Standards and Practices", unwritten rules, regulations and expectations for both parties: dating exclusivity, unimpeded availability in/out of school, unquestionable loyalty, and strict conduct concerning the opposite sex, right on down to How to Ride with Your Steady. And, of course, the greatest requirement of all: THSRWATNEBTFATOAOTCTTRO, i.e. The-High-School-Ring-Worn-Around-the-Neck-Exclusively-by-the-Female-as-the-Outward-Acknowledgement-of-Total-Commitment-to-the-Ring-Owner; sexist by today's standards, but hey! This was January '62.

Because the Ring was the Thing, it presented a problem if my emotional leap to hyperspace was going to work at all. You see, the Class of '63 would not be receiving our rings until mid-May, five light-months away. Arrrgh! What to do? Well, unbeknownst to my big sister, she rode to the rescue. Away at college, she eschewed her old high school ring (*how gauche!*), she was attending *The University*! So there it sat, loitering in her jewelry box in her vacant bedroom. Problem solved! I'd give Lauren *that* ring until ours arrived! That way we could, *"Let them see your love for me, and let them see by the ring around your neck."* Thank you, Elvis!

The only thing left was getting Lauren to say "Yes".

You might think all the warm fuzzies generated between us from the Roaring Twenties Dance to the picnic to our Daily Walks and Talks would make this a slam dunk, a no-brainer, a smooth move even someone with my clunky, Pure Adolescent savoir-faire could pull off. But confidence and self-esteem are rarely found in abundance, cruising on the same over-heated blood vessels that are also carrying the ingredients found in Clearasil as well as nature's own testosterone. She could say "No", although it would more likely be, "No, but thanks for asking" . . . the same thing I say when someone offers me brussels sprouts, only without the shouting.

With the Ring Issue semi-resolved, I really thought I'd be able to sell the arrangement. OK, it was my sister's ring, a downer for sure. But it was only *temporary*; after all, May being *only* five months away, was not really an *eternity*! (At least seen from that perspective.)

One thing stumped me: what to do about the chain? According to the unwritten rules, it wasn't compulsory. Some girls actually wore it on their finger; being the guy's ring, it would usually fit over the girl's ring. While looking moderately painful, some girls did do it that way. This being my sister's smaller ring, the chain thing would only be in order to strictly abide by the THSRWATNEBTFATOAOTCTTRO Standards and Practices -- which was different from the "unwritten rules". I think.

Guys did not tend to dwell on such matters; the girls had it all down anyway and any course corrections could be made ex-post facto. As long as they understood it, we were OK. I think.

To finish The Plan I had to, well . . . *finish The Plan*. When, Where and How was I going to pull this off? It wasn't like the movies where I could wait for just the Right Moment at the drive-in and pop the question (See *Grease)*. I probably could have set it up to double with Rich and Ann to actually go to the Totowa Drive-In but something this serious, this significant, this romantic was best done in private. Plus, selfishly (or insecurely) if she said "No," or "No, but thanks for asking," or "Oh My God*! Hell no!*" I wouldn't want anyone see me melting into a blob of slobbering protoplasm.

I finally noodled it out.

Over the weeks we had been in our Old Routine, I had managed to bob and weave to Lauren's new locker with a little more than our 20 minutes to spare before the buses left. Her locker was close to one of the stairways to the second-floor classrooms. I could meet her and we could run upstairs. By then, everyone with lockers up there would have headed down to the buses and we'd have the whole hallway, maybe even an empty classroom, to ourselves. I'd pop the question and, if everything went according to hopes and dreams, give her the ring, enjoy a celebratory kiss (or two) and still make it to the buses in time.

With the Where and How done, When was only part left. As it turned out, by the time I had resolved to Ask the Big Question, the calendar easily solved that one for me: Valentine's Day was just a week away. How perfect was that? So I "borrowed" my sister's ring and began planning the perfect way to get Lauren to say "Yes!"

And so it came to pass . . .

On Wednesday, St. Valentine's Day, 1962, with thumping heart, sweaty palms, and my sister's purloined ring, I met Lauren at her locker. We had already exchanged smoochy Valentine's cards that morning so nothing could get in the way of The Plan. When the locker door closed and she spun the combo lock locked, I took her hand and said, "I have to show you something really important!" and hurried us off to the stairs. Lauren came along with some hesitancy, more out of curiosity than reluctance.

"Where are we going? What is it?"
"It's a surprise."
"Where?"
"Up here."
"Up here? Your locker isn't up here!"
She had me on that one but we were almost to the top and in the hall.
"Hang on. We're almost there."

And then we were. Standing alone. No kids. No teachers. Just the two of –

Blam!

The door to the Bio Lab banged open and out came Mr. Bjorn Krause, biology teacher and my brother's biggest fan; Craig had been in his class his senior year, 1959. One of my brother's talents was drawing. When Mr.

Krause assigned drawing the cross section of a leaf or the cut-away view of a frog's leg, Craig's work was always "Textbook Quality". Mr. Krause never passed up an opportunity to mention big brother's homework art since I was now in his class and, from childhood, couldn't color within the lines even with numbers. My leaves and worms were more Picasso to my brother's Audubon, much to Krause's disappointment. Where my brother's worm looked almost photographed, mine looked Cuisinarted.

"Brian! Hello! I've been meaning to ask you, how's your brother, Craig? Doing well in...where did he go?"
"Hello, Mr. Krause. He's fine, thanks. He's up in Maine at Bates College."
"Right, right . . . well, tell him I said hello and how much I miss seeing those fine sketches he used to turn in."

Tick-tick-tick

"Yes, sir. Will do."
"That's quite a talent your brother has, you know? Does he intend to follow a career that will make use of it?"
"Well, he's always wanted to be an architect, sir."

Tick-tick-tick-tick-tick-tick-tick

"Excellent! Excellent! I had hoped he would have pursued something in zoology or botany. With his artistic ability, he would have been a real asset to any school's science program, perhaps an illustrator for a biology textbook company."
"Yes-sir-I'll-be-sure-to-tell-him-sir."

Tick-tick-tick-tick-tick-tick-tick-tick

"Well, you two better get moving or you'll miss your bus. See you in class."

"Yes-sir-you-bet-ok-right-tomorrow."

The stairway doors closed behind him.

Lauren didn't have Krause for Bio and had been waiting patiently, equally aware of the *tick-tick-tick*.

Of course, I hadn't anticipated getting ambushed by my brother's fan club. If Lauren said "Yes", I didn't want this magic moment to end on the sour note of seeing our buses leaving without us, having to call Mrs. Sills for a ride, and having to explain why. Definitely un-cool. Lauren's smile was about half-power. Obviously, something was up, but . . . what?

"OK, what are you . . . what are we doing here?"

The smile remained but a blend of coy suspicion and touch of exasperation crept into her voice.

The halls were empty, Krause and the teachers now definitely gone. Not even a janitor in sight but we were still whispering which made it seem as if we were planning some giant conspiracy! The Big Moment had arrived.

"Lauren, ya know . . . we . . . I mean . . . since . . . umm . . . it will be a few . . . um . . . months before . . . well actually it won't be *months* . . ."

This was not going well. Not even close. Where was the soft lighting? Violins? Chorus? The things I intended to say had shredded into bits of script confetti whirling around the wind tunnel of my muddled brain. I was feeling like a blithering idiot. Hell, I was *sounding* like a blithering idiot! This was supposed to be . . . *romantic.*

I put down my books, put down her books, took both her hands, looked into to her questioning eyes and said, "Look-I-know-this-may-be-a-little-early-since-we-aren't-getting-our-rings-for-another-five-months-but-I-don't-want-to-wait-that-long-so-I-borrowed-my-sister's-ring-until-May-so-I-could-ask-you-now-if . . . you would go steady with me?

Because of the buses, I knew it couldn't have been the hour that seemed to pass as she said nothing, just looking up into my eyes, and then that smile came like a sunrise shining from her face. She squeezed both my hands then let them go and brought them up to my face and pulled me down to her lips and gave me the most – (*what?*) enthusiastic, no -- Passionate? Yes, *passionate* kiss ever! She held me and her kiss for a long, tingling moment, then pulled away slowly, her eyes still closed as if savoring the moment and then, with her hands still on my face, smiling her megawatt smile, looking right into my eyes and said with growing emphasis, "yes, Yes, *YES!*"

And I put my arms around her and hugged her and she stood on her toes and hugged me back and laughed her soft laugh and with my head buried in her curls, said something heartfelt and meaningful that sounded disturbingly like, "Klaatu Barada Nitko!"

Then I reached in my pocket and pulled out my sister's ring and immediately picked up her quizzical look. I had gone over the part about my sister's ring so quickly to get to the Big Question, she hadn't caught everything I said. So now I'm a little embarrassed and trying to explain how it belonged to my sister but she didn't wear it anymore because she was in college and it would be OK with me if it was OK with her if she wore it until our rings arrived and then I'd replace it with my ring and . . .

"Of course it's OK! I'm just glad you finally asked me!"

Another moment I will never forget. Ever.

Conveniently, Lauren was wearing a thin gold chain around her neck with a charm on it. Only as women can do with jewelry and certain articles of clothing, she had the chain off, the ring on the chain and the chain back around her neck in an instant.

Then she did it again! Put her hands on my face, pulled me down to her lips and kissed me quickly as if sealing our clandestine little ceremony! As she pulled back from the kiss, her hands slid down my arms to my hands and squeezed them and then with that smile said, "We're gonna miss the bus!"

Whoa!

And off we went, down the stairs and out to the buses -- Lauren leading the way, still holding my hand. I didn't have to run; Lauren was towing me along behind her like a Macy's Parade balloon. Of course, we made it. Barely. No time (or place) for another kiss (dammit). Just my "I'll call ya later," and her, "I can't wait!" And off we went in opposite directions for what was a float-on-air ride home. No school bus in the civilized or uncivilized world of motor vehicle transportation ever rode like that again.

Home. Of course I called. We talked, I laughed, she giggled and we talked some more. We may have had many senseless, pointless conversations but that one was the Mother of Them All; the phone lines must have been loaded with nitrous oxide. At 16, neither one of us had cultivated the vocabulary for serious *Sweet Nothings* (Brenda Lee, 1960). But we felt it. Then all of a sudden, "I gotta go!" I hadn't been tracking how long we'd been on the phone but it seemed way shorter than usual to say goodbye.

"Uh-oh . . ."

"Wha . . . Why? Is something wrong?"

"No! Nothing's *wrong*! I have to call Judy and Joan and everybody and tell them the news! I'll see you tomorrow! Bye!"

Click. Dial tone. Oh yeah -- that.

Despite my less than eloquent verbal skills and adrenalin fueled motor-mouthing the question, she said *Yes*! Lauren of the Dazzling Smile said *YES*! I was happy she was happy we were happy. Life had been good. Now life was great! World Peace was at hand! Just 17 long, grueling hours until I saw . . . My Steady! And didn't that have a nice ring to it!

Steady As She Goes

By the next morning, The Word was out: Lauren was Going Steady with Brian.

When I arrived at the Senior Door, Lauren was surrounded by Flag Twirlers and Field Hockey teammates, a small crowd that attracted others who hadn't yet heard The News. As I got within range, one of the girls noticed, said something to the group and the covey scattered – except a smiling Lauren. Around her neck, the gold chain, and the (borrowed) Ring.

"Hi!"

"Hi!"

"Quite a crowd . . ."

(Giggle) "Everyone's excited!"

"Cool! Me, too!"

"C'mon!" I said with feigned exasperation; taking my hand, we started the walk to her homeroom. Now, it was generally considered indecorous to Hold Hands during school – unless you were in an Established Relationship. Which we were now. There was The Ring right there. As we walked and small-talked, there were little interruptions from her friends, a nudge punctuated by a giggle or some other Secret Girl Language. Of

course, I acted oblivious to it all – but I wasn't; I got the drift. And it added a Glow of Approval seeing her friends were happy for her.

Once at her homeroom, Lauren went to her desk and I appropriated the one to her right. I can't recall now who sat there but he was consistently late – probably sitting next to *his* Steady several homerooms away. I think we zoomed past each other after the Second Bell which signaled the "Romeo Sprint" for guys in Established Relationships and other Lotharios to haul ass to *our* Homerooms before the Final Bell, the official start of the School Day. The Track Coach could have made great use of that time, just scouting the halls and recruiting.

The Big Question asked and happily answered, we settled into our New "Established Relationship" Routine, not that much different from the Old "Just Dating" Routine except for my sister's stand-in Ring and all the Proprietary Significance it announced to the world, on display there on Lauren's blouse. We soon made some minor adjustments.

For example, our buses arrived almost simultaneously each morning at Wayne Senior High. For reasons unknown (the Invisible Hand of Mr. Sills?), that gradually changed and Lauren's bus was pulling in as much as 15 minutes before mine. We agreed to forego her loitering across from Principal Van Dyken's office near the Senior Door and just meet at her Homeroom. With the extra time, she could put the finishing touches on homework or do some last minute cramming. Part of the "Protocol for Going Steady (Guys)" was escorting your Steady Girl to her next class; depending who was taking what at which period could make for some serious timing issues. Eventually, we blew off those classes that were geographically inconvenient and agreed just to rendezvous at whichever were closer. Of course, I still walked Lauren to the bus and still called her every day after school. When football season ended, we segued into meeting at the basketball games, staying for the Post Game Victory Dance (victory or not). Invariably, we would catch a ride home with Rich and Ann.

I should mention here our lives apart from school and dating had substance and dimension. Lauren's Flag Twirling, Field Hockey, and Girl's Gymnastics took up a lot of "after school" time throughout the school year. Playing the saxophone since fifth grade and being in the dance band in prep school, I put together a Dave Brubeck-type quartet of piano, drums, bass and sax with the help Kit Ebersbach, Class Genius and my best friend from elementary school. At least once a week, we'd get together for rehearsal, usually at the drummer's house because hauling a full set of drums around for a rehearsal would have been a mega-hassle. And anyway, his folks also had a piano.

Like the beer commercial: It doesn't get any better than this!

The Really, Really Big Event finally arrived April 5th when I turned 17! Lauren and I didn't make any special birthday plans because another friend, John Hinck, agreed to give me a lift after school to the local office of the New Jersey State Department of Transportation to secure my personal Key To Freedom: a New Jersey State Driver's License! With birth certificate and Social Security card in hand, I scribbled through the forms, took the Eye Test and was outta there in record time with my prize!

Finally!

Now, it wasn't really *the* "Driver's License"; it was a Learner's Permit, meaning you could only drive with another licensed driver with you. After 30 days, you would go back to the NJDOT office and take the dreaded driving test: driving around a Test Course with an Official State Testing Officer checking off your proficiency (or not) at a variety of driving maneuvers. Stories about those dudes were legion and all bad! It was said they would pass any attractive girl even if she couldn't parallel park (that's not actually 'driving' anyway). Indeed, girls who failed this part miserably still got a passing grade; guys could flunk if their hair wasn't combed. As a former Well-Mannered Preppy, I did not anticipate any problems. Being raised on a farm, I already had plenty of experience driving tractors and trucks. The big thing was: in 30 days, Lauren and I would be able to go out on *actual dates* without having to double with Rich and Ann or anyone else. Those awkward and very uncomfortable times being chauffeured To and From by a Parental Unit would be over and done, done, *done*!

Come on May 6th!

One of Life's Great Truths: Time passes differently when you're young. A week can be an eternity waiting for your Driver's License or fly by to a dentist appointment. Being with Lauren, time pleasantly drifted along; not too fast, not too slow. We were able to be with each other long enough to make anticipating the next time almost bearable. I don't know if Lauren felt that way or not; we never had conversations about existentialism, neo-impressionism or the French Revolution; even Austrian economics missed our radar somehow. I just assumed from her big smiles, warm welcomes, hugs, kisses, and holding hands, she was as happy and excited about "us" as I was. It was right about then I started to think about "Being In Love". What was that all about? What did it feel like? Being with Lauren always felt good, happy, giddy, warm, exciting. Was this *love*? Were we *in it*? It sure felt bigger than being in *like*! But for all the things we did talk about, we never talked about that. We never said "I love you" to each other. But it sure *felt* like it.

I'm reminded of lines from the Barbra Streisand hit *The Way We Were*, *". . . Misty water-colored memories, of the way we were . . ."*

Thinking now about then, it's hard to pull a sharp focus. Every memory is in watercolor; a soft gossamer kaleidoscope of images changing shape; times, days, parts of days, different scenes, crystal clear sometimes then blending into no distinct picture but a familiar image just for a moment, then separating and blending again.

". . . Can it be that it was all so simple then? Or has Time re-written every line . . . ?"

If I were to chronicle our "day to day" days together with an attempt at continuity, even with the profusion of *"scattered pictures of the smiles we left behind . . ."* pigeon-holed into *"memories . . ."* I'd likely be more wrong than right about which pictures went with what days. But no matter. Even with a forgotten fact or added fantasy, the recollection of our time together remains as wonderful, thrilling and heartbreaking as it actually was.

"What's too painful to remember, we simply choose to forget . . ."

What happened next isn't misty or water-colored at all. It is as clear and sharp and painful to remember and as unforgettable as if it happened just now . . .

That Look

Lauren wasn't just a Great Smile on the face of a cute girl. True, whenever we were together, she always appeared right on the verge of a smile or a laugh as if anticipating something fun was just about to happen. The brightness would dim a little when something thoughtful that passed for "serious" came up. But Bright, Cheerful, Happy . . . that would be Lauren day to day. Not giggly or hyper just . . . well, Bright Cheery and Happy! At least when I was around. But I have to say she did have *That Look* when "not pleased", a combination of emotions wrapped in an expression. Not quite a frown or a scowl, she would purse her lips as if having tasted something unpleasant; then came a gray cloudy overcast blocking all that sunshine. *That Look* was reserved for something really annoying, irritating, disappointing, unwanted like a huge load of weekend homework or people being intentionally un-cool, spoiling a good time. A lot of Unpleasant was wrapped up in *That Look*! While I can't say I ever saw her angry or heard her speak sharply to anyone, *That Look* alone spoke volumes.

On this particular gorgeous spring day in May, *That Look* was nowhere in my mind. The sun was blooming! The birds were shining! The flowers were singing! Lauren and I were Going Steady *and* I just passed my Driver's Test! I now possessed that most cherished 2"x2" Official State of

New Jersey document: the driver's license! I was State sanctioned for Driving Solo! No parents, brother or licensed friends! Just Lauren, me, and my mother's car come this weekend! In just a few weeks, we would be celebrating our "First Anniversary", one whole year since that miraculous blind date and that first kiss! And the second! And then there was the Junior-Senior Prom next month! (*Reminder to self: need to ask her; Going Steady or not*). Nope -- it couldn't get any better than this!

And I was about to find that out.

It was a Tuesday. Thanks to Field Hockey, family matters and the usual intrusions of teenage life in general, we had been literally out of touch until Homeroom this morning.

At this point, my dad, a mechanical engineer, was head of the New York office for his company based in Minneapolis. Thanks to his clout and her years of experience, mom worked as his Office Manager. Together, they drove into Manhattan every morning leaving mom's car all alone, begging for attention. And with my new Certified NJDL, I was just the guy to give it! Driving to school instead of riding the bus was a major deal back in '62. Of course, I had to park in the Junior Class Parking Lot; Seniors had their own lot, closer to the Senior Door, the main entrance to Wayne High. But Senior Year was just four months away and then this would all be ours! By then, maybe Mr. Sills will have had a change of heart -- or heart transplant – and Lauren could ride with me every day.

As luck would have it this day, my new motorized independence was stifled by my old school bus. Having to take a detour due to some local road work, the Yellow Snail pulled in front of me on my regular short-cut and actually *did the speed limit* all the way. By the time "we" got to school, parked and made it to Lauren's Homeroom, there were just a few minutes before the First Bell.

But there she was. At her desk, book open, reading as usual. The desk to her right, empty as usual and I plopped down in the comfy wooden seat. As usual.

"Hey! Good morning! Great to see you! Sorry I'm late. I got the car but then I got stuck behind my old bus! Can you believe it! It didn't go over 12 miles an hour the whole way in! Maybe 13 downhill . . ."

(My penchant for Gross Exaggeration always got a grin if not an outright smile; a great way to start the day!)

Not today. Not this morning. Here's where a water-colored memory morphs into an HD video.

Lauren is looking down at her book, elbow bent, her cheek resting in the palm of her hand as if holding her head up. Strange. She doesn't look up. When I pause, instead of that dazzling morning sun smile I've come to love, she looks over at me with *That Look.*

Uh-oh.

Women have the corner on the intuition thing alright, but seeing *That Look,* even the most obtuse male could tell something was seriously wrong. Sharp as a blimp when it came to women and their vibes, even I could tell something was happening and the "something" was not good.

"Hey! What's wrong? What's going on? Why the look? Are you OK?"

Silence. Just . . . *That Look.*

"What? Have I done something wrong? Did I forget something?"

After a couple of those seconds you measure in light years, she reached out her hand like she always did and I almost passed out from relief. Everything was OK. Something or someone else had bothered her before I arrived.

I reached for her hand as usual but -- it wasn't her open hand. She was holding something and as she opened her fingers, she handed me my sister's ring. Staring at the ring, then to Lauren. *That Look.*

Fear. Dread. Panic.

"Wha . . . what's this? What's wrong? What happened? What did I do?"

Heart pounding. Sweaty palms. Mind racing between This Can't Be Happening and What Have I Done?

"Lauren, what is it?"

My answer was first bell going off and the room erupting as everyone started making their moves for the start the school day.

Me, trying not to shout . . . "Lauren, what is it? What have I done?"

And Lauren of the Dazzling Smile looked away, closed her book, slipped it into her book bag, then turned back to me. No more of *That Look.* No expression at all actually. She just folded her arms against her chest, right where the ring had been, glancing down as if assuring herself it was really gone. Then finally turning to me and, in that same clear, soft voice but this time without any expression or emotion, just matter-of-factly said, "I don't think we should go steady anymore."

Like an exclamation point at the end of her sentence, the final bell rang. The guy whose seat I occupied came running through the door. The rest of the class was settling in. Lauren's Homeroom teacher, Mrs. Harding said, "Mr. Wilson, shouldn't you be in your own Homeroom now?"

I stood. Lauren didn't look up. She was busy re-arranging things in and out of her desk. I started to say, *"Hey! I'll meet you later and we can talk, OK?"* But the class was getting quiet, waiting for the Morning Announcements over the PA and I didn't want everyone to witness the tragedy unfolding right in front of them.

So I hurried out, glancing back when I reached the door to see if Lauren might . . . but she didn't.

Stunned.

Like a zombie, I tried navigating my way down the hall to my locker. What just happened? *This was crazy!*

"Hey, Wilson!"

Great. It was The Big O, the not-so-pet name we had for Mr. Otis Grady, arch-typical Vice-Principal. Huge. Mean. Hall Sheriff. Keeper of the Clock and Punisher of Hall Stragglers.

"Running a little late, aren't we? Actually, I see we're not running at all! Do we have a problem this morning?"

Ordinarily, I would have had a bunch of smart-ass answers for him. But that morning, I just mumbled something humble and kept going to my locker. When The Big O was out of sight, I turned for the EXIT door, walked to the car and drove home.

Confused. Dazed. Scared. I felt the ring in my pocket. What just happened? Had I had lost her? Really?

All the way home, then sitting in the empty house, I kept going over everything since Friday. What could I have *done*? What happened Friday when we last saw each other? A quick kiss goodbye, "See you Monday . . ." that was all, right? We didn't even talk on the phone. Was that it!? Did I forget to call? No! She couldn't talk anyway. She was away. Right? Right! So what was it? Had I said something stupid? Had I done *something*? Blank. Nothing. No answers. Hell, maybe I didn't have the right questions! Was she sick? Yes! No, she was in school. Wait . . . *was there someone else*? No, couldn't be. If she wasn't in class, Flag Twirling, Field Hockey, Gymnastics Team or home, we were together. Jealous! *Was she jealous?* Impossible. Jealous of whom? I barely knew any of the other girls in our class anymore except Lauren's friends and they would usually disappear whenever I showed up. They weren't my type anyway. Even if they had been Miss June, August, and October, flirting with other girls when you were going with someone was like committing adultery. Besides, everyone knew I was Going Steady in a Committed Relationship with Lauren.

I was *in love* with Lauren.

As much *in love* as a 17-year-old can be.

At 17.

Meaning as much as a 17-year-old *thinks* he understands what *in love* is.

At 17.

I thought I knew what *in love* felt like. Is this what *break up* feels like?

That afternoon, bordering on desperation, I drove back to school, timing it to get there before the 2:30 bell that ended classes for the day. I would simply meet Lauren coming out of class or at her locker and we'd talk this through. Murphy's Law: Road Repair traffic. The bell was ringing as I sprinted across the Junior Parking Lot. I knew I wouldn't make it to Lauren's last classroom, so I headed for her locker instead. It was closer anyway, so that was in my favor.

Dodging, weaving through the jam of kid traffic, I kept looking for her face just in case. Nope . . . Passed our meeting place at the Senior Door just in case. Nope . . . Ah! There she was! At her locker! Nope! That was the girl whose locker was *next* to her locker. Out to her bus! I'll wait for her there. And I waited until the doors closed and the bus pulled away. She never made it.

Wait! It was Tuesday, field hockey practice day! I *knew* that! But the morning trauma had blown it right out of my mind. In its place was this Demolition Derby of Desperation, Denial, and Delusion! And Hope.

Proms and Yearbooks

Strange how mind and memories work. The line hadn't even been written in 1962, yet when I first heard it 32 years later, I blinked and there she was: Lauren of the Dazzling Smile . . .

"Hope is a good thing, maybe the best of things, and no good thing ever dies." The Shawshank Redemption

I started walking to the practice field. If we could just talk. If I could find out what happened, I could make it right and everything would be OK again.

I made it halfway. Seeing the bevy of identical, form-disguising white gym suits all scampering about, waving their hockey sticks, trying to pick out which was Lauren, came an early flash of what became my LOS (Logical Operating System) which concluded: this was dumb. I wasn't about to have a meaningful conversation about our fractured relationship with Lauren in her gym suit, at field hockey practice, surrounded by teammates. And the coach. How dumb was that? Leave now. Call later.

So I pulled an about face. Back to the car and back to the farm.

Not only did I not make it to the practice field, I didn't make it to the phone either. It was not for trying. I dialed her number two, maybe three dozen times -- but hung up each time before it rang. Fear of rejection is one powerful de-motivator.

For the rest of the week, I would get to school and -- as casually as possible -- slowly drift by her homeroom door. Sure enough, there she'd be, at her desk, head down, reading or writing. Thankfully, no one else had taken my old spot, the vacant seat at the desk to her right. Altering my routes to class, I would see her in the halls with her girlfriends, talking, laughing – no worries. Meanwhile, I was being emotionally whipsawed: happy she wasn't with some other guy; miserable she wasn't with me.

A hallway poster reminding Juniors and Seniors about the Prom gave me the inspiration and excuse to make the call. I'd invite her to the Prom! The Junior-Senior Prom was a big deal: evening gowns and special hair-dos for the girls, white dinner jackets and carnations for the guys; the Ultimate Dating Event and Social Scene of the School Year. Since it didn't appear Lauren ditched me for another guy, she would say *"Yes"* and we could iron things out that evening!

When Friday arrived and the time I always called, most of my earlier confidence had evaporated. What if she wasn't home? I'd have to speak with her mother. And say what? *Hi, Mrs. Sills . . . it's Brian Wilson. You remember, the guy who used to go steady with Lauren before she ripped my heart out when she gave me the ring back? Right. Well, not really very well at all but . . . how about you? Mr. Sills still his cheerful self? Say, as if you didn't see this coming: is Lauren available? Oh, not home yet? Hmm. OK. Message? Oh sure! Will you please ask her if she would go to the Prom with me? And could either one of you call me back with the answer? Or should I call back in the next life?*

Right.

But I couldn't wait any longer. Getting a prom dress and hair appointment is *uber* more involved than renting a tux and getting the same old haircut. Take a deep breath and make the damn call. Hey – remember, just last week at this time you were in an Established Relationship with this magnificent girl!

Ouch.

With all the muster-able courage and resolve I could scrape from the bottom of my barrel of intestinal fortitude, I did it. I dialed her number. One ring. Two rings. (If she was home, she always made it by the second ring.)

"Hello?" (*There it was, that clear, soft voice . . . this was it. Here she was. Speak. Speak!*)
"Hey! Hi-Lauren-it's-Brian-how-are-ya?" (*Oh yeah - real casual*)
(Long pause)
"Hi . . . Brian."
(*I was just calling to say you ripped my heart out and I haven't been able to stop thinking about you trying to figure out what happened; why you broke . . . why we aren't . . .*)
"I was calling to ask if you would go to the Prom with me next month?"
(Long pause)

(Yes! Yes! Oh, I'm so happy you called! I was such an idiot Monday! I'm so sorry if I hurt you. I know I hurt you. I saw you in the halls a few times; it was all over your face but I couldn't . . . Yes! Yes, of course, we're going to the Prom. And, if you don't mind, I'd like the ring back to wear with my new dress!)

"Oh . . . well, I already have a date. Roger Blecch is taking me."

(WHAT? Roger Bleccch? The short guy with that mouthful of braces? How . . . where the hell did he come from? When did he ask? What about us? What . . . Roger Blecch?)

"Oh . . . Well . . . OK." *(Lauren what the hell happened? What did I do? Not do? Say? Not say?)*

"Thanks for asking me."

"Right. You're welcome. See you at school."

"OK."

"Bye."

"Bye."

And she was gone.

Maybe a minute on the phone and not just rejection but – *Roger Blecch*? I had long reconciled that I was not Mars' Gift to Venus but I didn't think I had been whipped with the Ugly Stick either. At least I didn't have Metal Mouth. And after all those kisses and smiles and hugs and laughs, how could they have all been just tossed aside, discounted, forgotten in just one weekend? According to the 1962 Moral Code for WASPY Teens, the absolute worst thing I could have done was try to come on to her in some . . . inappropriate way. Going Steady, the worst thing I could have ever said was we needed to Go All The Way. That never happened. Not even close. I never even had the thought. So what could it have been? Nothing. Nothing else. Nothing that couldn't have been worked out, talked out, understood. Dammit, *we were only 17!* How complicated is Life at 17?

I didn't go to the Prom. There was no one else I wanted to be with; there was no Second Choice. Up until a week ago, going with Lauren was certain. I had nearly forgotten the courtesy of asking. Wait! Was that it? No. Couldn't be. Could it? No. No way. It was six weeks away. I knew other guys who planned on going (and actually went) but hadn't asked anyone yet. That couldn't be it. *I just couldn't figure out what it was.*

Remarkably, at dinner that evening, out of nowhere, my mother asked if I was taking Lauren to the Prom and had I made arrangements to rent a tux?

"No."

"Well, you better hurry. Your brother had to go all the way to Rutherford to find a tux for his prom because he waited so long."

"I won't need a tux. I'm not going."

(In typical mom fashion) "What? Not going? Of course, you're going. What happened to Lauren? Isn't that her name?"

"Yep, that's her name and no, I'm not going."

Uncharacteristically, my father jumped in, "Wait . . . Lauren . . . isn't she your girlfriend or something?"

"She *was* my girlfriend. She broke up with me this week."

"Broke up? What, did you get married or something?"

Dad was finding this amusing.

"No, Dad, we were going steady and on Tuesday she gave me my ring back."

"A *ring*? You bought her a *ring*?"

(Sidebar: While my father and I never enjoyed the warmest, closest father-and-son relationship -- he reserved those attentions for my brother -- he didn't have a habit of being whatever the term was we used back then for "asshole". End sidebar.)

"No, dad, I didn't buy her a ring. I bor . . . forget it."

(Sidebar again: Things like this were never discussed in the Wilson household. Not boyfriends, not girlfriends, love, sex -- none of that was part of dinner or any other conversation. For everyday Boy-Girl stuff: read *Dear Abby*. For details on sex: see *The Secret of Life*, a small hardcover book that mysteriously appeared in the bedroom right after Mom discovered my brother's *Playboy* collection under his mattress. The medical school cross-section drawings of the male and female genitalia, along with the full-frontal anatomical drawings of Fallopian plumbing, a "cervix" and "uterus" were just too damn confusing to the 14-year-old eye without some serious adult guidance. That wasn't about to happen on the post-Victorian, Episcopalian, Uptight WASPY Wilson Farm. There were perfectly good books to handle all that rather than The Big Talk. Eventually, Biology, senior year Health classes and personal experience filled in the blanks. My father taking a sudden interest in my social life was both unexpected and unnerving considering the feeble grasp I had on my own feelings, freshly shredded just a few hours ago. End sidebar again.)

"Wait. You said you *borrowed* a ring? Whose ring?"
"What is this, Dad? The Spanish Inquisition?"

Anyone overhearing all this might have surmised Dad was "just kidding" but "anyone" wasn't me. And I was on the verge of losing it. Before I said some things that would cross the Parent-Child Respect Line, I stood up to leave the table. Glancing at my mother, I saw her shooting daggers Dad's way. He dropped it; nobody spoke. I went upstairs to my room, slammed the door, turned on WABC and pretended to do homework. Nothing was ever said about this by anyone. *Ever.*

Sometime before I fell asleep, a part of me came to terms that Lauren and I were done; that it was highly unlikely, right next to impossible, I would ever get the answer to *Why*, much less a reconciliation.

The other part of me though totally rejected this finality. In desperate optimism (aka adolescent naiveté) I would continue to believe there was still Hope. There was a reason, not a good one, but some reason for Lauren's decision. If I could just find it out, everything could be alright . . .

September and Senior Year arrived soon enough. After a summer working a part-time job as a waiter and short-order cook at the now-gone Anthony Wayne Charcoal Ovens, learning some of Life in the Real World, the first day of our Senior year arrived in all its autumn glory. It had been nearly five months since I'd seen or spoken to Lauren. During the summer, I dated some girls from towns around Wayne but they weren't Lauren. They had nice smiles, but not Lauren's. They had great personalities, but not Lauren's. They all kissed well; some *very* well. But not like Lauren. Still, I had managed to shake off most of the misery from the Prom call rejection. Not really. I just didn't think about it as much.

Hope may "spring eternal" but the Fates saw to it once again that Lauren and I wouldn't be sharing any classes. Or lunch period either. In fact, in a school the size of Wayne Senior High, you could go days, maybe a week or two, without seeing some people. And so it was with Lauren. Despite scanning the hallway traffic between every period, it was two weeks before I saw her. Suddenly. Unexpectedly. Where I never thought to be looking: the school library. Going in to kill time from an open period, there she was. Like a flashbulb, she just popped into my eyes from across the room, getting up from a table where she had been sitting with her usual friends. She was smiling that smile and laughing quietly, gathering up her books, obviously on the way out to her next class. I couldn't just stand there staring; someone who knew her was sure to notice. Teenage girls have their own special radar. I couldn't go back out in the hall, so I made my way as quickly and invisibly as possible into the stacks of books where she wouldn't see me. *Why did I do that?* It wasn't as if I was scared or guilty or something. Actually, I was scared. Scared that she would see me and look right through me. Or, worse, give me *That Look*. So I avoided her -- for our entire Senior year.

It wasn't difficult. I just stopped looking and the year zipped by. Whenever I did see her, after a sharp but brief stabbing pain, I noticed she wasn't walking with Roger Blecch or anyone else of the male persuasion. So the forever Hopeful side of me continued to Hope for a miracle.

April arrived with no such miracle. As the Prom posters started to go up, remembering my sacrifice the previous year, I determined I wouldn't miss this one. After all, you only get one *Senior* prom. And I was determined to ask Lauren. What could she say, No? Well, yeah. Been there; done that. But that's better than wondering if the miracle of her saying, "Yes" was missed because I didn't ask.

Logic and I were becoming pretty good pals.

Don't ask me how I did it or where the guts came from but nearly two months out from the Biggest Social Event of the Year, after school on a Friday in April, I drove home, waited the usual 30 minutes and dialed Lauren's number.

One ring. Two rings.

"Hello?" The soft, clear voice I hadn't heard in over a year floated over the same bedrock of fear, remorse, insecurity and regret from last time. But still with a smidgeon of Hope . . .

"Hi, Lauren, it's Brian." *(Wow! That sounded friendly, firm, self-assured; definitely not the mass of Jello I was feeling inside.)*

(Well! Hello! How are you? You haven't spoken to me in – why it's been our entire senior year! I know you didn't leave for that prep school again; I've seen you in the halls! And by the way, I thought you were hysterical in

"Visit to a Small Planet"! So what have you been doing? How's the band? Where are you going to college? We have so much to talk about!)

"Oh . . . hi." *(I can't believe you're calling. Again.)*

"How've you been?" *(Is that a note of "I can't believe your calling" I hear in your voice?)*

"OK. Fine. You?" *(I hope this isn't about the Prom.)*

"OK . . . fine . . . thanks." *(The bleeding from that gaping hole in my chest you made last year has mostly stopped, except when I've seen you in the hall or the library . . . otherwise, if I was any better, I'd have to be twins! A-ha ha ha ha . . .)*

"Listen, I don't want to keep you . . ." *(more than a couple hours)* "I just thought I'd get an early start and ask if you would like to go to the Prom with me this year?" *(There. That didn't sound too desperate, did it?)*

The Long Pause . . .

"Gee, thanks for asking but I already have a date." *(Rrrrriippp! There! Feel familiar? Now leave me alone. By the way, that looks like blood appearing on your shirt...)*

"Well . . . yeah . . . I kinda figured, but I had to ask! See you there." *(This is called trying to put a good spin on things.)*

"Yes. OK. Well . . . bye."

"Bye."

My date for the Prom was Judy Doremus. Her father was the Wayne's Chief of Police. We doubled with my buddy, John Hinck and his eventual wife, Barbara Johnson. When John told Barbara that Lauren said no and I might just take another pass on going, Barbara said I should ask Judy. Going Steady with Lauren, I didn't get to know many girls in our class. Why should I? And after you subtracted those who were also going steady and those you didn't know at all, there weren't a whole lot of options. Judy and I had some classes together. She was nice. Attractive. But there weren't any sparks between us. She accepted my invitation but I'm pretty certain she knew this would be our first and last date just so each of us could say *yeah, we went to the Senior Prom.*

Prom Day arrived complete with a rented white sports coat, tux pants, and red carnation. John picked me up in his '58 Chevy convertible -- much preferred over my mother's dorky Borgward station wagon -- and off we went to get Barbara and Judy, meet the parents, hear the parental sermons about safe driving, curfew, and hints of other prohibitions; the customary and compulsory pre-Prom obligations.

I got a glimpse of Lauren that night. Her date was a Junior I didn't know. Of course, she looked stunning in her gown and hair and all. But she could have been wearing a flannel shirt, combat boots, and a football helmet and I wouldn't have thought otherwise. Crowded as it was, sitting at different tables across the room, we were never close enough to make eye contact. Seeing her dancing the slow dances with Some Guy was hard. But it was over soon enough. Everyone left for post-Prom parties, nights of legendary debauchery, drunken revelry and lost virginities.

John drove back to Judy's house and I walked her to the door (Chief Doremus peering thru a curtain; must be related to Mr. Sills). We kissed the perfunctory Prom-obligated good nite kiss, chastely of course which we would have done even if the Chief hadn't been lurking behind the drapes.

"I had a nice time, Brian."

"I'm glad. Me, too."

"See you at school."

"Yeah, see you at school."

"Goodnite . . ."

"Goodnite."

And that was it. The Senior Prom, "Ultimate Dating Event and Social Scene of the School Year" was over. You could say Lauren and I went together -- just with someone else.

After the Prom, classes were pretty much a joke; everyone cramming for Finals, counting the days that were left; after Finals, daily rehearsal for Graduation Day. Somewhere in-between, the Wayne Senior High Yearbook, *Embers 1963*, arrived. This, too, was a Very. Big. Deal. Except for the Super-Secret Yearbook Committee, no one knew what pictures of whom doing what had been collected, screened and included, memorializing our Glorious Senior Year! Everything from big plays at football games to candid shots of teachers and students, teachers and teachers, students and students, would be in there. And, of course, the individual pictures of graduating seniors, taken at a local studio, proofs reviewed and worried over by student and family until The One was chosen to be the Pictorial Memorial, the permanent black & white Memory of Your Youth, your friends and your high school "career" that would bring back its own Shock and Awe, laughter and sadness at reunions years later.

I don't know how it went at other schools but at Wayne, yearbooks got passed out and passed around to friends, classmates, teachers and staff for signatures over their pictures along with pithy comments like: "2 Good 2 Be 4gotten", encouragement: "Good Luck at (College Name)", promises: "Always stay in touch". Mostly, you'd write over your picture: Person's Name, Snarky Comment, Your Signature. Close friends would write Name, "See page 129" and signature, telling the Yearbook Owner where to find something special that took more space to write than would fit in the margins around your wallet-size picture. The back pages, where ads had been sold to supporting area businesses to defray printing expenses, had plenty of white space for the Signee to scribble more profound comments of Deep Meaning.

All this took time. Not everyone was available to sign when your Yearbook was available. Often you would find yourself surrounded by people you hung with and the signing became slow and furious.

Sitting in the auditorium waiting for Graduation Day Rehearsal to start again, I just had my Yearbook snatched away by one of the fellow cast members from the school play when a clear, soft voice behind me said, "Brian?"

I turned into the mega-watt smile of Lauren, standing over me, thrusting her Yearbook toward me with both hands. And with that cheery tone sounding as if she was thrilled we were still together, just gone to the Prom or just returning from a date, she said, "Will you sign my yearbook?"

The etiquette here was to say something like "sure and you sign mine", each handing their book to the other. This Yearbook Reciprocity completed, each could then go out in search of whoever was still as yet Unsigned. It also gave the other person something to do while you were scribbling your sentiments and vice versa. But mine had disappeared and hadn't made it back yet.

"Hey, Lauren! Hi . . . sure, I um . . . mine is gone . . . somewhere and . . ."
"That's OK. Don't worry. I'll catch up with you and sign it later. Here . . ."

With Lauren's Yearbook in hand, a rush of what-to-write angst overwhelmed me. I couldn't write, *"It was fun getting to know you this year! Good luck, Brian"* or *"You'll never know how much I wanted to kill myself after you broke up with me, Best Regards, Brian"* or some clichéd drivel you wrote when you had nothing else to write to someone you were never really close to. But without my Yearbook to keep her busy, I wouldn't have time to write what I wanted to write while she just stood there, waiting. I thought if she got the sense I was writing the equivalent of *War and Peace*, that would create a very awkward moment. For me, anyhow. Standing there waiting, occasionally waving to a friend or chatting with one who came by, Lauren appeared her happy, cheerful self.

It was clear she wasn't suffering anything like I had been since That Day -- and was going thru at that moment.

Right then, one of her best friends came up to her, handed over her Yearbook and said, "Sign!" They both giggled as Lauren went to a nearby seat to write something more than "Stay in touch!" I flipped to my picture and wrote, *"Lauren, See page 148. Brian."*

In all that white space, I poured it out as best but as succinctly as I could. Over the years, teachers told me my penmanship was the closest thing to Sanskrit they had ever seen; even *I* could hardly read it an hour later. But that day, in those few minutes, I strained to do my best to be more legible than any other time in my life. All the while, I kept one eye on Lauren's progress which didn't help my legibility.

As it happened, we finished at the same time. She closed her friend's book and handed it back; I closed Lauren's and handed it back to her while she kept talking with her friend. My Yearbook was still MIA.

I interrupted them with, "Sorry, I don't know where mine got off to . . . why don't . . . "
Lauren just glanced at me and said, "Thanks! It's OK. I'll get yours later. Just come find me."
"Sure. OK."

By the time my wandering yearbook found its way back, rehearsal was starting up again and everyone had to take their assigned seats. By the time it was over and the subsequent mad rush for the door, Lauren was nowhere to be seen.

She never did sign the Book.

I've often wondered what she might have written. *"Good Luck in college!"* or *"I'm so sorry I hurt you. Let's meet during the summer and see if we can patch things up. Call me."*

For having just turned 18, I was getting a great reputation among myself for being quite the dreamer. At least I could claim a rich fantasy life.

And then it was Graduation Day. Pomp and Circumstance. Out on the football field, the Class of '63 sat in the bleachers, two segregated rectangles of jubilant teenagers, robed in school colors with matching motorboards: blue for the guys; white for the girls, tassels fluttering in the summer breeze. Pithy Podium Drivel from whoever was speaking. Then the line-up, grads alphabetically arranged, stood and filed down from the bleacher seats, up the steps to the platform. As your name was read to the assembled multitude of family, friends, and strangers, you walked across the stage, executed an awkward but hearty handshake of "Congratulations" from Principal John Van Dyken as he simultaneously handed you your diploma, then walked off stage and back to your seat. Brian, Diane and Donna, the three unrelated Wilsons in the class had a long wait. Then the Closing Congratulatory Comments, followed by the much rehearsed simultaneous Tassel Move, then whistles, hoo-rays, a few tossed mortarboards, the rush of family, friends, flashing Polaroids and Kodaks and that was it.

Finis.

The End.

So long, high school; Hello College.

No more pencils! No more books!

No more teachers' dirty looks!

No more Lauren either.

Or so I thought.

The Razor Blade of Life

Tom Lehrer, one of the great iconoclasts of the 1960's pop culture, wrote satirical songs that had a comparatively small but rabid group of fans. As a college student and budding radio DJ, I counted myself among them. One of his most popular ditties was *Bright College Days*, a salute to the pursuit of higher education. This chapter's title comes from the last verse:

"Soon we'll be out amid the cold world's strife, Soon we'll be sliding down the razor blade of life. Oooo! But as we go our sordid separate ways, We shall ne'er forget thee, thou golden college days."

Lauren went off to some college in South Jersey I had never heard of. By now, like emotional rust, time was slowly but inexorably eroding any hope of seeing her again much less rekindling that indescribable tingle. Yet, she was never totally, *totally* gone from my mind. And I never totally, *totally* lost some small measure of hope that might be more accurately called fantasy. Still, there was a life to live, college to experience and law school to accomplish. Plan your Work; Work your Plan! Carpe the Diem!

And beware whatever the Diem might have hidden behind Door #3.

On reflection, it never ceases to amaze how easily, how quickly the unholy trinity of Time, Circumstance and Fate can derail a simple plan.

In as few words as possible, here is a brief synopsis of a My Simple Plan and Its Derailment:

After my freshman year, living at home, commuting 30 miles to the Rutherford campus of Fairleigh Dickenson University, I transferred to Louisiana State University. *(Why LSU? That's a story in itself, but it has nothing to do with Lauren so I digress.)* In October, I met Sharon (on a blind date, no less, to an LSU football game). We dated. We hung out between classes. We did homework together at my apartment. We got pregnant. We got married. And I never made it through Law School. Just ten years after Lauren, I was married with four kids and a big time Baton Rouge Radio Star with several other business interests. There are some great stories within the stories of How, What and Why all that happened, maybe to be told in some other life. But more significantly, by 1973, a year after the arrival of Wilson #4, it had become abundantly clear Queen Kong (my on-air name for Sharon) and I were not nearly as compatible as the production of four children might imply. Almost daily, the handwriting was scorched upon the walls of our humble abode that debunked the wisdom of couples staying together "for the sake of the children"; our coupling would be uncoupling sooner rather than later.

Back to the story of Lauren . . . but first, some relevant history . . .

On my birthday, April 5, 1968, during the obligatory "Happy Birthday" call from the farm, my mother mentioned a letter had just arrived, addressed to me. Naturally, being the youngest with no adult standing despite having been her only offspring to have made her a grandmother, she had already opened and read it and informed me it was a note from the

Wayne Senior High School Class of '63 Reunion Committee announcing our Five Year Reunion. Instantly, and for the first time in some time, Lauren appeared in my mind and I wondered, *what if she was . . .* well, no matter. Regardless of the When and Where, I wouldn't be going; couldn't go, actually. Work, staff seniority and vacation schedules already posted at the radio station wouldn't accommodate the time off. With the pending arrival of Wilson #2, money was tight so flying was out of the question. Of course, despite being huge with child, Queen Kong would have insisted on coming along which doubled the already impossible cost. Driving might have been an option but considering a four-day 2,600-mile round-tripper in her condition was an Instant Spoiler. As requested, I RSVP'd regrets along with a requested address change. A mere five years later, a similar letter arrived announcing – (what else?) the *Wayne Senior High School Class of '63 10th Year Reunion*. The vision of Lauren returned for an encore, but again, and for many of the same reasons, I had to send regrets. A few years later, my new CPA, Bert Potter, also Class of '63 and still a Wayne resident, told me Lauren was a no-show for both the 5th and 10th reunion. Strangely, I felt that same sense of relief along with the recurring fantasy she might be single, then came the free-floating memories of her, us, Going Steady and the unrequited "everything else". With things rapidly deteriorating at home, I often found myself asking that face full of shaving cream in the mirror, *"What if . . . ?"*

We did go back to Wayne in '73, just not for the Reunion. At different times over the years, part of the family vacations was spent driving from Baton Rouge to New Jersey for Mom and Dad to get their quality time with the grandkids and vice versa; the folks flying to Baton Rouge was never an option. My parents had an inexplicable prejudice against The South in general and a visceral hatred for Baton Rouge, its infamous humidity in particular. Of course, there were other issues, but again, I digress.

Beginning with this trip, the 10th year Reunion missed by *thatmuch*, Lauren would pay my mind a visit every hundred miles or so; Baton Rouge to Wayne is 1,355 miles. Sliding slowly but inexorably down Tom Lehrer's razor blade and closer to the Marriage Exit sign, imagination passionately wrapped its arms around memory and, with Lauren's vision riding along beside me, created spectacular scenarios along with improbable but enticing possibilities; the "What If" kaleidoscope made the jump to warp speed.

As we were coming into Wayne, I impetuously made a slight course correction and took the more circuitous route to the farm, one I had often taken after Lauren had handed back the infamous Ring; a route that would take us past Lauren's house. Would she be there? Could my timing be so exquisite I would get a glimpse of the 28-year-old vision of her? Of course, Sharon had no clue about my re-routing. She knew we were close to the farm but her attitude was just like the kids, "Are we there yet"? To be honest --- and this is a *true* story -- my last-second turn wasn't that impetuous at all.

We came up on the turn for Black Oak Ridge Road from the opposite direction of the farm. The green shingled split-level house with big trees in the yard was still the same; SILLS in block letters on the mailbox was reassuring. The driveway empty. A lamp bulb glowed behind the opaque white curtains covering the picture window. Was she there? Was *anyone* there? No way to tell, I drove the remaining 10 minutes to the Wilson farm.

Three days later, a Sunday, when we left for the long slog back home, I retraced the less direct route. This time, a green Mercury Cougar was parked in the driveway. Was that Lauren's or had Mr. Sills uncaged a repressed youth in some mid-life crisis and splurged on a *Cougar*? Unlikely. Maybe it belonged to Lauren's little sister. She was certainly old enough to drive; probably in college by now. I coasted by slowly for a good look as well as to accommodate the STOP sign at the corner. Without X-ray vision, nothing like Lauren -- or anyone else -- could be seen clearly through the gauze of the curtain except the outline of what had to be the world's longest burning light bulb glowing through the fabric.

Oh well . . .

I made the turn with one last glance over at an empty backyard (can't be too sure) and off we went, back to whatever the Fates had waiting in Baton Rouge, four already squirming kids, the dour Queen Kong and the bright, exciting vision of Lauren sitting beside me, fading little by little every hundred miles or so.

This became my routine every subsequent trip to the farm: pass her house on the way up; pass her house on the way back. Occasionally, the mysterious green Cougar was there; most times, not. Then one time, the day before we were to leave for Baton Rouge, running to the store for my mother, there was a green Cougar, turning onto Ratzer Road out of the

Route 23 traffic circle, coming toward me! I tried to get a look as it was passing -- and *there she was*! In the passenger seat! Wasn't it? Must have been her little sister driving! But wasn't that Lauren smiling, laughing? And then gone . . . faster than it took you to read it . . . *just-like-that*. I thought I'd get whiplash or a heart attack from the rush! If only I could have snapped a U-turn! But it was too late; I was already in the feeder lane for the circle. Could I believe what I saw or saw what I wanted to believe? Certainly, Ford Motor Co. made more than one green Mercury Cougar. But what were the chances of one carrying two young women, one of whom was . . . could have been . . . might have been . . . ?

This Changes Everything

When we left the next day, I took the now customary re-route. We passed the house I had secretly dubbed the House of the "Burning Bulb" (Portrait of a Light Bulb Thru a White Curtain). No movement. No sign of life. And No Cougar. Had it *really* been Lauren? Was it really *the* green Cougar? Does the mind, emotionally whipped, surrounded by bickering kids and a hostile wife, staring down hundreds of butt-weary miles, desperate for a quiet place, lit by the memory of an indescribable smile and warmed by a soft voice, play tricks on you? Or did some of that illegal weed enthusiastically inhaled during notorious panty raids and off-campus parties, fry some important brain cells?

I replayed and rewound and replayed those seconds in my mind for every one of those 1,355 miles back to Baton Rouge. Pulling into the driveway, hours, miles and words later, I still didn't have the answer.

About the same time three years later in 1976, everything changed

By then it had become crystal clear: Sharon and I were definitely *not* "made for each other". We had made the common mistake of many young people in heat, deluding ourselves into thinking the frequency and novelty of our off-campus sexcapades were True Love. Starting with a demanding college curriculum, then jobs and the intermittent and unintended Fruit of the Womb surprises, the next 12 years ground down the giddy College Romance part that was supposed to mature into the Deep Abiding Love part. At least, that's the Love Story most of our generation and social status had been told and sold; for us, it wasn't meant to be. For different reasons, eventually, separately, we each arrived at the same conclusion. Not that we shared it with each other, of course; that would have been too intelligent, too constructive, too mature. Emotionally and intellectually the stage was set. It would be one more year before it all ended.

In the spring of '76, Dad had brought his company to the brink of a Very Big Deal with a certain audio cassette manufacturer. To close it, however, required a field of expertise not available "in house" at the company HQ. Thanks to my broadcasting experience and cassettes being the New Big Thing, I was just the "expert" they needed. So for the first time in my life, my Dad called me for help: would I come to New York, meet with the Corporate Big Shots to help consummate the deal? Shortly after regaining consciousness, of course, I agreed.

Due to the prevailing circumstances with Queen Kong, it was arranged that Matthew, our oldest, and I would drive to the farm so he could get in additional quality time with the grandparents as well as a mega mano-a-mano road trip exclusively with the old man. D-Day arrived and we departed on the now very familiar trudge to The Farm. Once in Wayne, I took the "new normal" route with sadly predictable results.

Two days later, The Big Deal was done and I was a momentary hero. This required a Celebratory Dinner at The Triangle, the Wilsons preferred restaurant in Pequannock which, incidentally, required two more cruises past the Sills' "Burning Bulb". One could say, "The light was on but no one was home." Apparently.

Another two days and Matthew and I were to begin the drive back which now was going to feature an overnight stop in Washington at my sister's apartment; she had landed a high-profile job in the Nixon White House. Matt could visit his aunt, his aunt could visit her nephew and the old man could pocket a few bucks previously designated as Motel Expense.

The day before leaving, Dad's deal done and the pressure off, I thought of Lauren, my disintegrating marriage and how many more trips I might make to New Jersey. The folks were making serious retirement noises with typical Florida overtones. With no farm/grandchildren excuse to make the 2,600-mile round-trip drive, there would never be any chance or hope of possibly getting even a fleeting glimpse of Lauren again.

It was the reality of that finality that brought on the epiphany. With this smidgeon of uncommitted time, instead of sitting around moping, wondering, feeling sorry for myself, why didn't I just drive on over to the House of the "Burning Bulb", knock on the door and ask, "*Where is Lauren? How is Lauren? Any chance she's been trying to get my phone number? Don't you know who I am?*" OK, some of that might have been little over-the-top, but the epiphany was solid. Why wonder? Go! Ask! Find out! Easier said than done, Boy Wonder. Kinda like asking for a date to the Prom and that old fear of rejection. Let's face it -- there is safety in ignorance . . . but no satisfaction.

I thought about some self-fortification, like tossing back some of Dad's Old Forrester. Nah. The last impression I want to make at the door would be, "*Hi! Some drunk here asking about your daughter!*" And what the hell, I still had most of that *saviour fare* loitering around inside me, left over from the prep school years. That had worked pretty well 15 years ago. I'll make up some credible story that will make it appear perfectly natural for me to be there, asking about someone I had dated over a decade ago. No one would seriously have second thoughts about that, right?

Right?

Cold feet, doubt, worry, and embarrassment be damned! If I had come this far, this often, this circuitously -- and obviously I had -- this was my last chance, my only resort. With Matt and the folks fortunately distracted, I grabbed the keys, jumped in the new kid-hauling Dodge Maxivan and headed for unchartered waters.

Oh, and I did "borrow" some of Dad's Liquid Courage!

Being a Sunday afternoon, there was none of the never-ending weekday traffic and I pulled into the Sills' empty driveway in a matter of minutes. Déjà vu of the Night of the Blind Date was overwhelming. I hadn't been *here* in . . . ? Whatever. This was definitely not the time for poor math skills. Exit the van, deep breath, walk with confidence to the front door, actually a summer screen door now in front of the front door, pressed the door bell and heard it chime inside. Footsteps. Or heart beats? Both. The door swung open and -- just my luck -- the backlit outline of Good Old Warm and Friendly Mr. Sills.

Swell.

"Hi, Mr. Sills . . . you may not remember me, I'm Brian Wilson . . . my folks have the farm over on Ratzer Road . . . (*no response*) . . . I . . . um . . . ya know, I don't get to Wayne very often these days . . . missed the 10-year reunion a few months back, soooo . . . I was just kinda making the rounds to check up on friends with whom I graduated to, ya know, see how they were doing . . . "

Silence, long pause . . . and then, "Lauren is married and living in South Jersey."

Well! Thank you so very much, you cantankerous old fart! Not, "Why, hello, Brian . . . nice to see you again. What are you doing these days?" Hell, no. Just the facts, nothing but the facts crap. You know, I didn't come here to molest your daughter this time either, you hemorrhoid. Why not just slam the door, you . . .

"Is that Brian Wilson . . . ?" (*A rustle of clothing, the sound of approaching footsteps, another backlit figure: Lauren's mother. I'd recognize that voice anywhere.*)

"Hi, Mrs. Sills!"

"Well, Brian!" (*Punctuated by an elbow moving Mr. Wonderful out of the way.*) "Come on in! It's so good to see you again! My! Haven't you grown into quite the handsome young man! Come in. Have a seat. What have you been doing these – what? – 13 years since you graduated?"

The house was exactly how I remembered it. Everything in the same place. The stairs that Lauren descended into my life, my heart, my memories that

May evening . . . all right there in front of me. I could almost see her appearing again. The furniture hadn't moved. The lamp was on. Of course.

We sat at opposite ends of the couch, turned toward each other. She smiling and taking in the new Adult Me; Mr. Sills wandered off into back room oblivion.

"So! Are you in for a visit?"

I repeated the same mild bending of truth I had just told her husband.

"Just cruising through, some business, see the folks, missed the reunion, trying to catch up . . . how's Lauren?"

She hesitated just a little; a small cloud quickly passed over her face, her voice suddenly not as strong and positive . . .

"Well, she's just fine. You know she went down to Glasgow to college and got her teaching degree in Art. And while she was there, she met a young man. I guess they fell in love (*guess*?) and got married. She went to work as an art teacher and, like so many other young women these days, worked to put her husband through law school. They had a wonderful little boy, our grandson, Scotty; they come to visit every few weekends. He's such a joy! We just love him to death!"

Then what effervescence she had went flat. She lowered her voice as if not wanting Mr. Sills to hear and, looking down at her hands in her lap, said, "Of course, like so many young people these days, getting married so early . . . sometimes, you know, it just doesn't work out and she and Joe got divorced. I don't know now if she and Scotty will be coming up tomorrow or not."

Divorced? Divorced! Oh My God! Divorced! I couldn't believe it! Divorced! She's . . . available! I'm getting divorced! Is this possible! It's a miracle! God, I hope Mrs. Sills doesn't see me smiling in the face of what had to have been a terrible time for Lauren, for her, for them! I have to appear sympathetic not laughing and dancing and High-Fiving myself!

"Yes . . . um . . . wow that's . . . yeah, that's too bad. That's tough . . . I'm so sorry to hear it. (*Yes! Yes! Yes!*) So, um . . . is Lauren still working as an Art teacher?"

"Oh yes. She loves it so much. Scotty will be going to the same school next year and that will be a big help."

"So, um . . . (*here it comes*) . . . where in South Jersey does she live?" *(Am I being just too damned obvious?)*

"Bridgeton. It's a small town. Smaller than Wayne. But Scotty's other grandparents have a big farm nearby and they've been a big help through all this. But what about you? Tell me! Where are you living? Are you married? Do you have any children? What are you doing? You were going to be a lawyer, right? Are your parents still living on the farm? Tell me all about you!"

Mrs. Sills . . . still a hoot after all these years.

"Well, let's see. After Fairleigh, I transferred to LSU in Baton Rouge. Never made it to law school, I'm afraid. Like Lauren, I got married too soon. Had kids too soon. Through a remarkable set of circumstances it would take too long to tell, I wound up as a DJ on a Baton Rouge radio station. But everything turned out fine. Now I'm this big radio star in Baton Rouge and I own a few other businesses, so . . ."

"Well! Radio! That's certainly an appropriate career for you! I remember you were always so funny! And that great voice! I'm not surprised you're successful! So, children! Tell me about your children!"

"Yes, we have 4 of them . . ."

"Oh, my! FOUR! (*Typical reaction to "four", never the same for "three". "Four!" was always said as if you were a sex addict.*)

"Boys? Girls?"

"3 of each . . ." (*Big laugh, the line never failed.*)

"You're still so funny! You always had such a great sense of humor! What are their names?"

"Matthew, Samantha, Jennifer and Jeremy."

"Oh, what nice names! And what does your wife do?" (*Frankly, she makes me miserable, Mrs. Sills. We should never have gotten married. And we're going to be divorced any minute now. You're right, sometimes 'things' just don't work out. But maybe this time . . .!*)

"She works at Exxon Research Labs, looking for the Origin of the Universe or trying to solve for X or something." (*More laughs; Humor is such a great distraction.*)

We went on like that for a while. Questions about the folks, the farm, retirement, moving, all the time struggling to contain myself with Mrs. Sills' incredible good news Lauren was divorced!

I left in a cloud of promises to drop in and say "hello" to Lauren if she happened to come by tomorrow and, yes, whenever I was back in Wayne I'd be sure to drop by. She gave me a warm hug and a goodbye peck on the cheek and I was back in the van, back to the farm, riding high on a soft cloud of fantasies.

The euphoria lingered thru dinner and all the after-dinner small talk. Later, staring at the ceiling in my old bedroom that night, Matthew asleep across from me in what had been my brother's bed, I hatched the plan: on our way to Washington the next day, we would go to Bridgeton. This would be my best, maybe my only chance to see Lauren with any possibility of resurrecting some of those good memories, plant a seed until my own divorce came thru. And then . . . Plan Your Work; Work Your Plan!

And so it happened. After an early breakfast and all the good-byes, the Maxivan rolled out of the farm and out of Wayne, off to find Bridgeton circled on the map. Matthew was curious about the side trip. I told him it was some old business and wouldn't take long. If it did, there might be some kids around to break the monotony. Kids like Scotty. Naturally, I took the Alternate Route past the "Burning Bulb", just to make sure a green Cougar wasn't resting in the driveway. It wasn't.

It was a three-hour hike to Bridgeton off the Jersey Turnpike but we arrived after lunch. Lauren's address was listed in the phone book I found hanging in a 7-11 telephone booth.

I can't remember the street name now but we were on it, counting down the numbers until we came to a white one story duplex. There were a few cars parked on the street but no green Mercury Cougar. Oh well, I had never established it was actually *her* car anyway. I parked the van at the curb, and with Matthew sprawled out in the back reading a book, walked up the front door just like I knew what I was doing.

A note was taped to the window: *"Please come around to the side door"* with an arrow pointing left.

OK. I can do that . . .

Around to the side door. No door bell. Just as I was about to knock, another note taped to the inside glass. In what had to be Lauren's handwriting:

Scotty – I've gone shopping for a few hours. Get Grandpa to take you to the farm. I'll be by soon to pick you up. Love, Mom

Well . . . crap.

All this driving. All this time. All this conniving and noodling out a way to pull this off. All this emotional roller-coastering. And now this. Having come this far I wasn't about to give up now. We were in no particular rush. It was Sunday so traffic around the DC Beltway wouldn't be that big a deal so we would wait.

A block up the street was a gas station, closed Sunday, with a clear view of the door to Lauren's duplex. I drove up and maneuvered the van alongside some other cars, probably there for repairs, to watch and wait.

Unlike a lot of kids his age, Matthew was cool, not "are we there yet" antsy. He read his book and then fell asleep. I dialed around the radio, listening to various stations, eventually dozing off myself; the dying muffler on a passing truck woke me up. I had been asleep for almost an hour. A quick glance down the street turned up no sign of a green Cougar or any other car parked where one hadn't been already, and I could still make out the white speck that was Lauren's note on the back door.

I decided to give it one more hour or until Matthew woke up. Both happened almost simultaneously.

Now a little after four, I threw in the towel and my hopes and dreams with it. For all the good luck and good news, this Lauren and Me thing was just not meant to be. With a giant gloom cloud hovering over the van, we followed the NJ Turnpike signs back the way we came and pressed on to the Logic Free Zone, our nation's capital, and my big sister's apartment.

Matthew was excited to see so many of the famous buildings and monuments up close, happy to see his Aunt Stephanie and happier still to finally be out of the damn van. I couldn't blame him; the drive was butt-weary enough. The side trip had added more hours of that and for me, the crashing depression when Lauren failed to appear. Stephanie offered a soft chair, stiff bourbon, and some unexpected good news.

Mom and Dad had called. They were upset that Matthew's visit had been so short. Why didn't he stay with Stephanie while I headed back to Baton Rouge? Mom would take the train down the next day and they would "do" the Smithsonian and some DC landmarks, then return to the farm for general distractions and farm stuff with Dad. Whenever convenient, I would drive back to retrieve him, maybe bringing the other kids along. Was that a plan?

It meant clocking another 2500 miles but Hell, yes! Now that I knew where Lauren lived, this meant one more chance in just a few more weeks! Mrs. Sills hadn't said exactly how long it had been since Lauren's divorce but it sounded as if -- actually, I *wished* -- enough time had passed to see her, speak with her at a time when she just might be open to the idea of a new relationship. A new *old* relationship!

Optimistic or irrational? Whatever, Hope had returned for an encore!

This Is It

The Plan was accepted; Matt, Mom, Dad and Stephanie all thrilled. After an early breakfast before Steph and Matt headed over to Union Station to pick up Mom, I blew out of DC before the Beltway Morning Insanity got too far along and headed back home, solo. Three weeks later, the tailwinds of unbridled optimism, excitement, and high octane Fantasy blasted the Maxivan out of Baton Rouge and northward toward Bridgeton, NJ. Finally! This was it! The Trip of Trips! The ultimate realization of hopes and dreams that had been tormenting me for 15 years, now down to just a matter of miles and hours.

You know how sometimes you just *know* something? You just *know* you're going to get the job. You just *know* you're going to win the game. You just *know* something is going to work.

You just *know,* ya know?

Stoked! That's the word, the feeling, as I rolled into Bridgeton, winding my way back to Lauren's duplex. Saturday night. If she's not here, she would most likely be in Wayne. It's a Win-Win situation! Either way, *this time* it's gonna happen! *This time* all the doubts, questions, pain, frustrations, and fantasies will come to one monumental conclusion. *I am going to see Lauren. I am going to speak with her. I am going to tell her this story. I am going to tell her just how I feel. And I'm going to ask her straight out -- is there's any chance for us? And I am going to do this tonight.*

Coming down her street, past my former "look out" of the deserted gas station, the duplex was surrounded by cars. Something was going on. A party, maybe? Doesn't matter. Full Speed Ahead. Despite the crowd, I found a space nearby, parked the van and walked straight to Lauren's side of the building where all the lights and music were and up the side door. No note taped there this time. Through the window, bodies moving around what looked to be the kitchen. A perfect summer evening, the windows and doors were open, music and happy sounds spilling out from inside.

Just inside the screen door, I could see several people standing around, drinks in hand, yapping away. None looked like Lauren. Not knowing the evening's protocol, I knocked. Standing a few feet away, an attractive girl about my age turned immediately and pushed open the screen door.

"Hi! Come on in! Who are you?"

"Hi . . . my name is Not Invited, but thanks for asking."

She got it and laughed.

"Well, can I help you?"

"I hope so, I'm looking for Lauren."

"Lauren?"

"Yes, Lauren Sills, she lives here."

Laughing a little she said, "Well no, actually, *I* live here!" *(Uh-oh.)*

"Hmmm, OK but I was here just a few weeks ago and she . . ."

"OH! Lauren. LAUREN! Yes OK yes now I . . . yes, I know who you mean."

(Whew!)

"Yes, Lauren. She doesn't live here anymore. She moved a couple weeks ago."

WHAT! No! NO!

"OK then. Great. I . . . umm . . . I don't suppose you know where she moved?"

"Actually, yes I do. Just up the road, in Millville."

"Millville!? OK! Great! Thanks, any chance you know her address?"

"Oh gee, no, I don't. I did, but . . . well, we only met once when I came to look at the place and she was in a hurry so . . . but Millville isn't that big."

"Right. OK. Hey, thanks a lot."

"You're more than welcome!"

Then, as if she had a sense of what was going on, she called out "Good luck!"

OK. OK. Just a temporary setback, not a brick wall. Back in the van; check the map for Millville . . . Millville . . . there, about 10 miles.

The dashboard clock read 7:30 as I wheeled the van around and pointed it toward the metropolis of Millville. Lauren having just moved, I knew the phone book wasn't going to come to my rescue this time, but 411 will!

Even with Daylight Savings Time, it was more dusk than light when I came to a crossroad with a stop light. Looking around, a sign said, "Welcome to Millville". Well! This must be the place. Now to find a payphone.

Off to my left was the two-bay Millville Volunteer Fire Department with an annex which housed the Millville Police Station. Along the side of the fire station, there was a phone booth!

Bingo!

With no traffic or Millville citizens in sight, I made a perfectly executed illegal U-turn into the parking lot, drove up to the phone booth, jumped out and dialed 411.

"Directory Assistance?"

"Yes, in Millville, the listing for a Lauren Sills, S-I-L-L-S?

(*Pause*) "I'm sorry, in Millville, New Jersey I'm not showing a listing for a Lauren Sills S-I-L-L-S."

"It would be a new listing...she moved just a few weeks ago."

"No sir, I'm sorry, I'm not showing any listing under that name. Could she be listed under some other name?" *(Uh-oh.)*

"Yeah maybe, but I don't know it. Thanks."

It was possible she was still going by her married name. Mrs. Sills had mentioned it when she gave me the Big News that Lauren met, married and divorced some guy named "Joe . . . Xmplft", now an attorney she put through law school. The problem is I went deaf at "divorced".

Damn! Now what? No phone book listing, no 411, possible different name but she's living somewhere right around here. Maybe I could just drive around and see if I spot the green Cougar. What if she doesn't have it anymore? What if it never was hers? There must be . . . and there it was!

My solution was staring me right in the face! The POLICE station! Small town. Small town police. Everybody knows everybody. Certainly they'd know someone new who moved into town in the last three weeks. Risky maybe . . . but what the hell.

With Desperation leading the way, I walked to the door of the diminutive Millville PD. Interesting, my van was the only vehicle in the parking lot. Where is the Official Police Car? What if he was out on a call? The light was on inside. No note anywhere. Someone had to be "home". I tried the door, and sure enough, there was.

A cop who looked to have maybe 10 years on me was behind the counter shuffling papers. Behind him, a desk, a table and a couple chairs against the wall of a lone holding cell. Sparse but probably enough to handle any sudden crime wave they might get here in Party Town.

The cop looked up as I came in. Not surprisingly he looked . . . surprised.

"Good evening, can I help you?"

Out of sheer exhaustion -- or a poke from my sidekick, Desperation, I came out with it. All of it.

"Well, I certainly hope so. I've driven exactly 1,273 miles to see someone and now I can't find her. I thought you might be able to help."

After a pause, "OK, what's the name?"

"Sills, Lauren Sills, she and her son, Scotty moved here from Bridgeton sometime in the last few weeks but I didn't get the address. The lady who rented her apartment back in Bridgeton didn't have it either. I thought you might have noticed someone new in town. Saw the Police sign outside and here I am."

"Did you try calling Directory Assistance?"

"Yes sir, I just did. No new listing for anyone by that name. No listing at all."

"Maybe she didn't move to Millville. Or maybe she just hasn't gotten her phone installed yet."

At that moment, the door opened and an older guy with a gray beard, carrying a box which was obviously a chess or checkers came in, glanced at me, then at the officer.

"Hey, Bill, come on in and get set up; I'll just be a minute."

"Well, the woman in Bridgeton was very specific about her moving to Millville. With her young son, Scotty, I wouldn't think she'd go a couple weeks without a phone."

Not knowing Lauren's married name had become a great big problem.

"The only other thing I know is her ex-husband is a major league attorney around here. His family owns a big farming operation outside Bridgeton if that helps any."

Whether it jogged the cop's mind or not, having all these particles of information didn't appear to be helping but my comment about "big time attorney" visibly registered -- and not in a good way.

Now assuming a more attentive and professional stance, the officer said, "Why exactly are you so interested in this woman? You said you drove, what? A thousand miles to see her; you don't have her address but you know her ex is well known around here but you don't know his name but you do know his folks have a big farm. Maybe you oughtta tell me the whole story.

I thought about that for a moment. Why not? Maybe he'd be sympathetic -- maybe sympathetic enough to not toss my ass in that little cell on Suspicion of Stupid.

"OK, this may take a while but here goes . . ."

For the next 15 minutes, I told Millville's Barney Fife just about everything you've read up to this point. I left out the parts about my doubts, dreams, wishes and fantasies and gave him the "Joe Friday" version, "just the facts, nothing but the facts" . . . the revelation from Mrs. Sills, my earlier stake-out at the gas station and my approaching divorce. I ended with the truth: what it meant for me to see her, talk to her, to ask if there might be something there.

Sometime before I finished, the cop signaled his disinterest. He had gone back to shuffling papers, preparing to put an end to this Official Business and move on to the evening's chess game that Bill had set up and was waiting patiently to start.

"Well, sorry I can't help ya. Wish I could. Good luck."

And that was it. I was dismissed.

He turned away, stepped over to the chess table, pulled out a chair and, as if I had already left the building, began chatting with Bill.

What started in Baton Rouge on a supreme high, just crashed and burned in this tiny police station in the Lilliputian village of Millville, NJ. It doesn't take long to come down from such a high, but I wasn't about to break down inside a police station. That would be *prima facie* evidence I was Certifiable; men in white coats carrying a jacket with extra-long sleeves wouldn't be far behind. So, deep breath . . .

"Well, Officer, thanks for the help." And I was out the door into a suddenly oppressive humid summer evening and climbed into the van.

From "stoked" to "stunned" is the only way to describe the moment. All this time, the miles, the effort, the risk. And dreams. What now? Wayne was absolutely my last chance. Whether there was a green Cougar in the driveway or pink Sherman tank, I would absolutely be accepting Mrs. Sills' invitation to "drop in whenever you're in town".

This isn't over until I say it's over.

Now recharged with my New Semi-Delusional Resolve, I fired up the Maxivan and headed out the parking lot to make the final three hour push up to Wayne.

Already focusing on my new strategy, I almost missed it. Out of the corner of my eye, a movement. Standing backlit from the open door to the Police station, Bill with the beard was waving at me, waving me over to him.

Uh-oh. Was he the Police Chief? One of the White Jacket guys? Am I about to become a "Guest" of Millville?

I kept the van turning in his direction, pulled up near the door and cranked down the window. Bill walked over and leaned up against the van.

"Hi, I'm Bill. I couldn't help overhear what you were telling Pete in there."

(I guess not. You were sitting six feet away and I've never been accused of being sotto voice.)

"I think I know that young lady you're looking for."

"Really?" *(Are you kidding me?)*

"Yes, she moved in next door to me a couple weeks ago. When you said her son's name, Scotty, I figured that had to be her. Scotty comes over and plays with my grandkids whenever they visit. He's a real nice boy. She seems very nice, too. I think she's a school teacher."

"Yes! She is! Art. She's an Art teacher! Well, this is great! Thanks a lot, Bill!"

Still no other vehicle in the parking lot; he must have walked.

"Do you live near here?"
"Oh yes, right down this street."

He pointed over my shoulder to a tree-lined street that would have been a right turn at the traffic light. I knew I was close!

"See that white car under the fifth street light?"

One . . . two . . . three . . . four . . .

"Yes, I see it."

"Well, that's her car, parked right in front of her place. She's gotta be home at this hour. Probably close to Scotty's bed time."

8:45 pm.

"OK! Alright! Well, Bill, very nice to meet you! Thanks so much! I'm going to drive down there and . . ."

"Don't bother driving! Might as well park right here and walk like I do. By this time on a Saturday night, there are never any parking places on the street anyway. Most everyone is home or has some company of one sort or another. If it isn't snowing or raining, I always walk up here to play some chess with Pete rather than lose my spot!"

"Right! Got it. Alright then. Park and Walk it is. Thanks again, Bill. Good luck with the game. Watch out for those rooks!"

Bill chuckled, turned, waved and went back inside Fort Millville to do board battle with Officer Pete, leaving me ecstatic and parking the van.

Still no traffic, I sprinted across the street, spring in my step, all had been saved! The trip, the evening, the dreams will all come true in just a few hundred yards after all! I had gone from Stoked to Stunned and back to Stoked in whiplash time! *I just knew it would all work out!*

Glancing at the houses that lined the street, I was reminded of that 1963 folk song, *Little Boxes*, *"Little boxes on the hillside, little boxes all the same . . ."* They were all alike. The sidewalk led to steps to another sidewalk to steps to a porch, then window, window, front door, window, window. Some porches had potted plants and rocking chairs, some had nothing at all. Lights were on inside most of them, windows open to the cool evening. The occasional whiff of freshly cut grass zipped me back to that picnic at Ringwood Manor, sitting beneath the tree, holding Lauren's hand, me kissing her, she kissing me back, me tripping over uneven concrete . . .

Whoa!

Losing oneself in memories on *this* sidewalk could be hazardous to your shoe and other things.

Stumbling along, passing thru the glow of the first street lamp, Reality jumped out of nowhere and mugged me. *What am I doing? Really? What. Am. I. Doing? All this time I'd been imagining everything turning out just fine, anticipating this great Fairy Tale Ending . . .*

I walk up the steps, music playing softly inside, floating out the open window. I knock on the door, a soft, warm voice calls out "Who is it?" I'm hesitant to answer. I don't want to spoil the surprise but I have to say something . . . what the hell! "Lauren? It's . . . Brian Wilson." Silence, then, "BRIAN WILSON?" With a pleasant surprise in her voice, hurried footsteps, the front door swings open and . . . there she is! "Brian!" Her smile lights up the porch, the steps, the neighborhood, the entire Free World! She looks magnificent! Time has been good -- no, great to her!

"What are you . . . how did . . . come in!"

And with that, she reaches out, takes my hand and pulls me inside.

And I damn near stumble face first on another chunk of ruptured sidewalk. That brings me back from the dream, back on the sidewalk. Three lampposts to go.

But what if that's *not* the way it is? What if . . .

I walk up the steps, music playing softly inside, floating out the open window. I knock on the door, a voice calls out, "Who is it?" I'm hesitant to answer. I don't want to spoil the surprise but gotta say something . . . what the hell! "Lauren? It's . . . Brian Wilson." Silence, then, "BRIAN WILSON?" in a distinctly unpleasant tone. Shuffling footsteps, the front door opens slowly, and there she is! "Brian!" No smile, instead, I'm getting The Look . . . she's 200 pounds beyond the cute, slender high school girl in my memories, straggly hair, blotchy, unpleasant complexion. Time and circumstances have not been kind to her at all. "Well, what the hell are you doing here? How did you find me? Have you talked to my mother? It's late and I don't have time for this . . ."

Hands on hips, she glares at me, waiting for answers . . .

I didn't need a chunk of concrete to snap me back to reality this time.

Since struggling that day for the nerve to confront her parents, I was suddenly having a serious crisis of confidence. Could *this* scenario even be possible? Of course. *No. Not Lauren.* Why not? It happens to other women. A child. A jerk husband. A bad marriage. A bitter divorce. *No, not Lauren.* She would never let her self-esteem . . . oh really? Why not? You haven't seen her in fifteen years! You don't know her life, what she experienced. What was college like? Her social life? Just how bad was her marriage? How badly did it end? What did she have to put up with? Admit it -- it's a *possibility*! OK. But I doubt it. *I have to doubt it.*

Two lampposts to go.

But what if . . .

I walk up the steps, music playing softly inside, floating out the open window. I knock on the door . . . a soft, warm voice calls out, *"Who is it?"* I'm hesitant, don't want to spoil the surprise but I gotta say something . . . what the hell! "Lauren? *It's . . . Brian Wilson."* Silence, then *"BRIAN WILSON?"* That pleasant surprise back in her voice! Hurried footsteps, the front door swings open and . . . there she is! *"Brian!"* Her smile lights up the doorway, the porch, the world! She looks magnificent! Time has been very good to her! *"What are you doing? How did . . .?"* Then there's a movement in the shadows behind her -- another body. *"Who is it, lover?"* *(Lover?)* Into the light steps this guy, and what a guy he is! He is so big, he has his own zip code -- tall, dark and devastating. Standing behind Lauren, he wraps his arms around her; it's obvious "lover" is not just a term of endearment. *"This is Brian Wilson, honey. He and I dated years ago back in high school. I haven't seen him since graduation. Come on in!"*

And with that, she reaches out, takes my hand and . . .

Snap.

I'm there. Standing on the sidewalk between a white Toyota at the curb and the steps, porch, window, window, door, window, window Little Box.

Lauren's house.

This is it. The True Moment of the Moment of Truth. There are no other choices. No other possibilities. Lauren is as beautiful and free as she is in my fantasy, a nightmarish "Doreen Grey" portrait of her former self or drop-dead gorgeous, living with some Magnificent Specimen who captured her heart on the rebound before I could even get in the game. That makes the odds one in three and not in my favor.

A U-turn at this juncture would be prudent. But when you're in love or just deluded, Fantasy trumps Reality.

No, you've gotta do this. One in three is better than zero in three. You've come so far. Put yourself through hell and back. Fifteen years comes down to the time it will take to walk up these steps, knock on that door and whatever happens next . . . happens.

Deep breath. Sweaty hands. Pounding heart. Weak knees . . .

I walk up the steps. Indeed there's music playing softly inside, floating out her open window. I knock on the door and a soft voice actually calls out *"Who is it?"* I hesitate, speechless. Can't spoil the surprise but my throat was so dry. Gotta say something . . . what the hell! *"Lauren? Lauren, it's . . . it's Brian Wilson."* Silence, then *"BRIAN WILSON?"* Surprise but an indescribable tone, hurried footsteps, the front door swings open and . . . there she is . . . *"Brian!"*

Epilogue and Other Things

Is that it? What happened? Is that "The End"?

I'll explain.

In prep school, one of our Classic Reading assignments was Frank R. Stockton's, *The Lady or the Tiger*. I never forgot it. Now 50-some years later, I've "borrowed" his idea for the ending. While the title alone may be self-evident, if you never read Stockton's story, you missed the depth and flavor of the emotional cross-currents in it. *Wikipedia* gives an excellent summary:

The short story takes place in a land ruled by a semi-barbaric king. Some of the king's ideas were progressive, but others caused people to suffer. One of the king's ideas was a public arena using a trial by ordeal as an agent of poetic justice. Either crime was punished or innocence was decided by the result of chance. When a person was accused of a crime, his future would be judged in the public arena before two doors. Behind one door is a lady whom the king has deemed an appropriate match for the accused; behind the other is a fierce, hungry tiger. The accused is compelled to select a door. If he chooses the door with the lady behind it, he is innocent and must immediately marry the woman, but if he chooses the door with the tiger behind it, he is deemed guilty and is immediately devoured by the tiger.

The king learns that his daughter has a lover, a handsome and brave youth who is of lower status than the princess. The king does not shirk from his duty to hold a tribunal, and the princess' lover is thrown into prison to await his trial in the arena. The princess, meanwhile, through intrigue and influence, discovers which door conceals the lady and which door conceals the tiger. Once in the arena, the accused looks to the princess for help, and she discreetly signals for him to choose the door on the right, which he does. However, it is unclear whether she has sent him to his death or to a marriage with a woman she resents as a rival. The author then departs from the narration, summarizing for the reader various facts about the princess' state of mind and her attitude towards the woman the king chose for the arena's door and challenges the reader to decide which door the princess indicated for her lover. The story ends with the famous quotation: "And so I leave it with all of you: Which came out of the opened door – the lady, or the tiger?"

While I wasn't Lauren's lover, the conundrum certainly applied that summer night.

How do you think it ended? Which Lauren actually appeared that summer night in New Jersey?

Was she the 30-something version of my beautiful Blind Date with the Dazzling Smile from high school a decade and a half ago? Divorced, free of a bad marriage and whatever emotional hell it put her through, she had had the time and strength to recover, move on and embrace whatever Life offered next, hopefully, me and us.

Or was she the once-beautiful teenager whose sparkle and smile had been snuffed by unfortunate choices, a bad marriage and an unconditional surrender to bitterness? The emotional cauldron marriage can often become and turn the deepest Love into Hate in short order. Mrs. Sills had indicated it was bad, just not *how* bad. Had it been *that* bad to transform Lauren into a shrew?

Or was she that spectacular young woman, appearing in the doorway like magic, whose beauty, personality and smile would instantly reduce any red-blooded American male to complete and utter devotion, and obviously had?

It could only be one, but which one?

The answer follows – if you wish.

If you don't want to know, if the dangling question is best left unanswered, more tantalizing than what the reality may be, stop here. The written word will always be available should your curiosity be unable to tolerate the suspense any longer.

Which Lauren was it?

While contemplating your choice, let me add there's so much more to the story of Lauren. The emotional see-saw from adolescent fantasy to adult reality; the whipsaw between logic and emotion; the tug-of-war between the prickling Anxiety of Not Knowing and the Fear of a Tragic Ending. What began as just a simple story of unrequited love, from adolescence to adulthood; two people "sliding down the razor blade of life" separately but together, had morphed into a chance of actually starting over, becoming a real-life love story for the ages!

"If we had the chance to do it all again, tell me would we? Could we? Memories, may be beautiful and yet what's too painful to remember we simply choose to forget."

Here is the end of the Story of Lauren.

At the beginning of the Story of Lauren, I wrote -- *And everything you're about to read is true.*

I should have written - *And <u>most</u> everything you are about to read is true.*

Indeed, most everything did happen just the way you read it. Aside from the occasional memory lapse, absent some cloying but unimportant minutia and maybe a little sprinkling of poetic license, the people, times, dates and places, conversations, events and, most importantly, the feelings are as accurate as I lived them and as precise as I remember them now.

As for those three different endings? Indeed they had galloped through my imagination that evening; a Cuisinart blending of logical deductions along with desperate fantasies conjuring the possibilities of what waited just down the sidewalk, up the steps, behind the door.

Here is how it turned out, what exactly happened that summer evening in a little village in South Jersey, remarkably now a half a century ago.

Let's go back to Fortress Millville after my unsuccessful catharsis with Officer Pete...

Already focusing on my new strategy, I almost missed it. Out of the corner of my eye, a movement. Standing backlit from the open door to the Police station, Bill with the beard was waving at me, waving me over to him.

Uh-oh. Was he the Police Chief? One of the White Jacket guys? Am I about to become a "Guest" of Millville?

I kept the van turning in his direction, pulled up near the door and cranked down the window. Bill walked over and leaned up against the van.

"Hi, I'm Bill. I couldn't help overhear what you were telling Pete in there."

(I guess not. You were sitting six feet away and I've never been accused of being sotto voice.)

"I think I know that young lady you're looking for."

"Really?" (Are you kidding me?)

"Yes, she moved in next door to me a couple weeks ago. When you said her son's name, Scotty, I figured that had to be her. Scotty comes over and plays with my grandkids whenever they visit. He's

a real nice boy. She seems very nice, too. I think she's a school teacher."

"Yes! She is! Art. She's an Art teacher! Well, this is great! Thanks a lot, Bill!"

Still no other vehicle in the parking lot; he must have walked.

"Do you live near here?"

"Oh yes, right down this street."

He pointed over my shoulder to a tree-lined street that would have been a right turn at the traffic light. I knew I was close!

"See that white car under the fifth street light?"

One . . . two . . . three . . . four . . .

"Yes, I see it."

"Well, that's her car, parked right in front of her place. She's gotta be home at this hour. Probably close to Scotty's bed time."

8:45 pm.

"OK! Alright! Well, Bill, very nice to meet you! Thanks so much! I'm going to drive down there and . . ."

"Don't bother driving! Might as well park right here and walk like I do. By this time on a Saturday night, there are never any parking places on the street anyway. Most everyone is home or has some company of one sort or another. If it isn't snowing or raining, I

always walk up here to play some chess with Pete rather than lose my spot!"

"Right! Got it. Alright then. Park and Walk it is. Thanks again, Bill. Good luck with the game. Watch out for those rooks!"

And this is what happened next . . .

I slipped the van into reverse to go park on the other side of the lot, away from the front door of Fortress Millville. But Bill didn't step back from the van as you would expect someone would do with that telltale little *bump* as the gears engaged. Our conversation had concluded on a *very* helpful note and now it was time to get on with it -- his chess game and my second blind date, this time with Fate.

So why was Bill still leaning against the van?

Excited, impatient and getting a little annoyed, I looked right at Bill and saw him still looking almost wistfully down his street toward that fifth lamppost while he remained stuck to the van; for him, our conversation wasn't over yet. Apparently, there was something else he wanted to say but wasn't ready or just didn't know how. Before the pause dragged on uncomfortably long, he said evenly, "Yes, Lauren is a wonderful young woman and a dedicated mother. She and Scotty moved in just a few weeks ago . . ."

Yes, yes I know. You've already said that.

Then he moved his head slightly, from looking down the street to looking directly at me. Without some accompanying tears or laughter, I've never had the talent to "read" any emotion in someone's eyes and now, there was no signal from Bill, no telltale twitch, squint or blink of a clue what was coming. But after a deep breath that sounded a lot like final resignation, he said evenly, "Yeah, she and her new husband are expecting their first child in just a few months."

He held my eyes for some long seconds, watching my reaction as the reality sunk in like a dagger slowly stabbed into the heart; seeing the slow-motion collapse of what could have been this great real-life love story crumbling before his eyes despite my every effort to appear stoic and unaffected. After some moments, without emotion, he shrugged slightly with what might have been a sad finality and turned away with his head down, saying, "Tell Lauren and Scotty I said hello," and headed back inside to the awaiting battle with Officer Pete.

Instead of ecstatic and anxious to make my way down past the five lampposts, hopeful with the thrill of realizing a life-long dream, I sat in the van stunned, bewildered and in some great pain. And then it all turned into empty. All options were gone. All the chances had been taken and, now, all the choices removed. There was no Lady and there was no Tiger.

With Bill's revelation, my adolescent optimism and adult fantasies defaulted to cynicism and sarcasm as again, I imagined myself sauntering down the street to the fifth lamppost, up the steps, music from the window, knock on the door . . .

"Who is it?" "It's Brian Wilson!" "BRIAN WILSON?" (That didn't sound like the voice I remembered but it had been a while.) Footsteps, the door swings open and, "Oh . . . Hi . . . you must be Lauren's new husband! Hey! Congratulations! Yeah, Bill, your neighbor, told me to say hello. Me? Oh

well, ya see, I dated Lauren a while back, in high school actually and . . . and . . . ya know what? I loved her . . . I loved her more than you could ever imagine. And I've been trying to find my way back to her for 15 years. I've driven over two thousand miles five different times just to get a glimpse of . . . just to tell her . . . just to ask . . . her mother? Yes, I spoke to . . . no, no she didn't mention . . . well, it was quite a while ago. So, expecting, are we? Well, congratulations! Putting Scotty to bed? Oh, OK . . . well . . . no, no thanks. I've still got a long drive ahead of me. Please, just give Lauren my best."

Masochistically, I played that scene over a few times until Logic clubbed my Emotion into submission: *Dude! It's over. It's really, really, really over. The End. Finito.* It's not ending like similar recent tragedies of the heart: *Love Story, Endless Love, Bridges of Madison County* or even Longfellow's *Evangeline* -- but it shares the pain of them all.

I wasn't about to make that "walk of the five lampposts" now. What for? It would be pointless, even rude to knock on that door. Selfishly, I wasn't going to get anything I had come for; the only thing waiting for me down that street was more pain. For Lauren, my surprise appearance would likely fall somewhere between a strange curiosity or a mild irritation, not to mention the reaction of her new husband and father of their pending child.

I called out to Bill just as he opened the door, "Hey, Bill . . . would you do me a favor? It's late and I've got a long drive, so I'm going to just go ahead and hit the road. But the next time you see Lauren, would you tell her you ran into this guy named Brian Wilson she went to high school with and that he said to say hello and that once upon a time, he was really in love with you. Would you tell her that?"

Bill paused and turned back a bit. I tried to see the expression on his face but the light from the jail behind him kept it in the shadows. With a voice that carried the tone of empathy and finality, he said, "Sure, I'll tell her."

And he went in and closed the door.

I swung the van out onto a road that was as empty as I felt, driving right through the solitary red light and headed north. At least the trip to the farm would be a few minutes shorter now that I wouldn't be making that detour past the green shingle house with the light bulb that glowed forever through the curtains.

Lost in that kaleidoscope of misty water-colored memories, minus the sparkle of hopes and thrill of fantasies, I don't know how but I made it to the farm that night and the end of the story of Lauren.

Brian Wilson is a nationally-known radio and television host, author, speaker and consultant.

Prior to moving into management, Brian hosted successful radio programs in several of the nation's largest cities, including New York, San Francisco, Atlanta, Houston, Baltimore and Washington, DC. As morning drive host at WABC/New York, he assisted the station with its transition from music to talk. As co-host of the highly successful Z-Morning Zoo at Z-100/New York, Wilson opened at Radio City Music Hall for two weeks of sold-out performances for world-famous entertainers Siegfried and Roy.

Wilson also played a role in the start-up of CNN, hosting an entertainment segment called *Take Two*. In a return to Atlanta in the 90s, Brian not only worked in talk radio, he also hosted *Talk at Night*, a weeknight television talk program.

As the founder of Vacation Relief, Inc. (VRINK), Brian was the first major-market talk radio host to fill-in around the country without leaving the comfort of his home studio. Wilson hosted radio programs in Seattle, Sacramento, Minneapolis-St. Paul, Kansas City, Dallas-Fort Worth, Charlotte, Atlanta, Baltimore, Washington, Philadelphia, San Francisco and New York, to name just a few of the cities.

Wilson is the author of three books – *Watercolor Memories: The Story of Lauren, The Little Black Book on Whitewater,* and *A Media Guide for Market-Liberal Organizations.*

Wilson was born in New Jersey and attended several schools on the East Coast. He spent his college years at Louisiana State University. He lives in Virginia with his wife, journalist Cassie Wilson, and their golden retriever, Nellie.

Made in the USA
San Bernardino, CA
01 January 2020